WITHDRAWN

THE *Truman Committee*

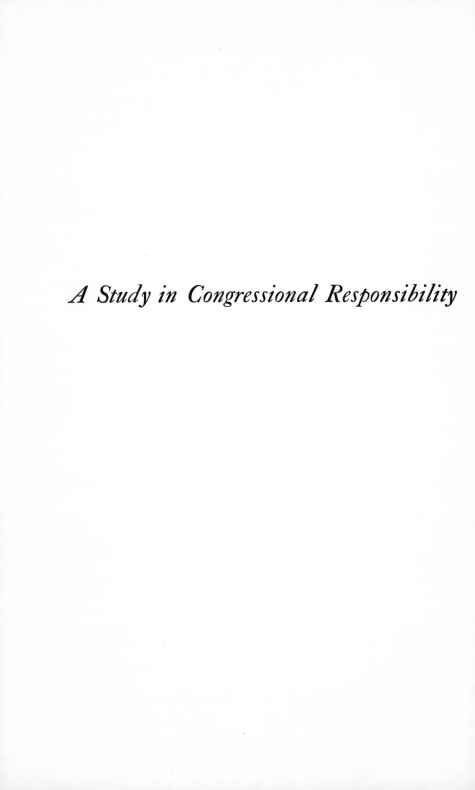

A Study in Congressional Responsibility

THE Truman
Committee

DONALD H. RIDDLE

RUTGERS UNIVERSITY PRESS
New Brunswick, New Jersey

for LEAH

Preface

The Senate Special Committee to Investigate the National Defense Program was the most important single Congressional committee dealing with the mobilization program of World War II. From 1941 until 1948 the Committee covered almost all phases of that program and exerted considerable influence on its course. The Committee was not only extremely successful, but it was also one of the most responsible investigating committees in recent history.

This is an examination of that Committee and its work, treated as a case study of responsible investigation. There are recent studies of irresponsible committees, notably the House Committee on Un-American Activities and several state investigating committees. But there are no comparable studies showing how responsible committees function to offer a standard of comparison.

There is an essential difference. One can establish at least a prima facie case of irresponsibility by taking a significant number of individual investigations by a committee and demonstrating that these have not met reasonable standards of responsibility. On the other hand, the case for a responsible committee must rest essentially on its work as a whole. In this study an effort has been made to show that the Committee's work followed a consistent pattern, and that the pattern was one of restraint and responsibility.

The major source for this work is, of course, the printed record of the Committee's work contained in its published hearings and reports, supplemented by its files on deposit with the National Archives. An important additional source, contributing whatever life this study contains, is interviews with Committee members and staff and with persons who were affected by the Committee's work. The writer is deeply grateful for the willingness of these persons to take time from busy lives to discuss the past and in some cases to make available personal files.

Professors H. H. Wilson and Marver Bernstein of Princeton University and my colleague at the Eagleton Institute of Politics, Paul Tillett, read the entire manuscript and made very helpful suggestions and comments, for which the writer is extremely appreciative. Rebecca Levin contributed innumerable improvements to the style of the final draft. And Carole McCloskey patiently and accurately typed several drafts of the manuscript. Needless to say, no one but the author is in any way responsible for whatever shortcomings remain.

No acknowledgement would be complete without mention of the incalculable contribution of my wife. She read and improved the style of several drafts, and her mixture of prodding, inspiration, and encouragement is responsible for the completion of the book by a writer with an unlimited talent for procrastination. The dedication is a totally inadequate gesture of appreciation.

Donald H. Riddle

Princeton, New Jersey
July 5, 1963

Contents

THE *Truman Committee*

Introduction

It is the proper duty of a representative body to look diligently into every affair of government and to talk much about what it sees. It is meant to be the eyes and the voice, and to embody the wisdom and will of its constituents. Unless Congress have and use every means of acquainting itself with the acts and the disposition of the administrative agents of the government, the country must be helpless to learn how it is being served; and unless Congress both scrutinize these things and sift them by every form of discussion, the country must remain in embarrassing, crippling ignorance of the very affairs which it is most important that it should understand and direct. The informing function of Congress should be preferred even to its legislative function. The argument is not only that discussed and interrogated administration is the only pure and efficient administration, but, more than that, that the only real self-governing people is that people which discusses and interrogates its administration.

Woodrow Wilson [1]

In March, 1792, during the first session of the Second Congress, the House of Representatives established a select committee, with power to call for persons and papers, to investigate the defeat of General St. Clair by Indians in the Northwest Territory. So began the first Congressional investigation. The St. Clair investigation has been followed by 600 or more Congressional investigations.[2]

There has been general acceptance of the legitimacy of Congressional authority to conduct investigations for the purpose of informing itself, controlling the executive branch, or informing the public. Even at the time of the St. Clair investigation Washington and his Cabinet recognized Congress to be an "inquest," vested with the power to conduct inquiries in the manner of the British Parliament. Their only concern at the time was that the separation of powers provided by the Constitution created some differences from British practice and that executive papers must be protected in the interest of national security.[3] In spite of the general acceptance of Congressional investigatory power, specific investigations have frequently produced concern that they were unrelated to any legitimate Congressional purpose, were infringing on the rights of individuals, or were usurping functions (especially the judicial function) which do not belong to Congress.

As a result of numerous contests of investigating committee powers in the courts, broad general limits on Congressional investigations have been established. These seem to be: [4]

1. Congress clearly has the power to conduct investigations as a necessary corollary of its legislative power. In doing so, it may compel persons to testify and to produce papers under threat of conviction for contempt of Congress, punishable by fine or imprisonment.

2. The power to investigate is not unlimited. It must be related to a valid legislative purpose under the Constitution. Furthermore, the witness must be made aware of the relationship between the questions asked and the legislative purpose before he can be compelled to testify.

3. The Constitution clearly limits the powers of Congress and hence limits Congressional investigations. Congress may not

usurp executive or judicial functions, nor may it abrogate the separation of powers; for example, it may not compel the executive branch to produce privileged documents. The Constitution also establishes protections for the individual which Congressional investigating committees must observe—particularly the privilege against self-incrimination. Furthermore, Congress is bound by the guarantee of due process, and the Supreme Court has indicated that there are at least some restraints imposed on a committee by the First Amendment's protection of individual rights.

4. The courts may review the conduct of Congressional investigations if justiciable issues arise.

5. Congressional committees may determine their own procedures virtually without restraint, for the courts have not been inclined to interfere with or review their procedures.

While the courts have clearly been willing to review the exercise of investigatory power and have repeatedly held that there are limits upon it, the established limits are very broad indeed. The courts have been reluctant to interfere with the functions of Congressional investigating committees, and they have presumed a valid legislative purpose. Only on rare occasions has the Supreme Court seen fit to reverse a contempt conviction.[5]

Within the limits set by the courts there is still room for a great deal of committee abuse of its investigatory powers. Individuals may be harassed—held up to public scorn and subjected to informal but nevertheless real "outlawry," loss of work or heavy expense in defending themselves. Congressional investigating committees may meddle with executive functions and even usurp the judicial function by exposing individuals in such a manner as to produce a public verdict of guilty. Consequently, the major responsibility for ensuring responsible use of the investigatory power rests with the two houses of Congress and with the committees themselves.

However, it is difficult to establish precise criteria for judging Congressional investigating committees. They are political bodies whose prime standard of success is likely to be political effectiveness. Beyond that, for the purposes of this study the following criteria are suggested with the understanding that they are somewhat subjective in nature and that there may be differences of opinion about the meaning of some of the terms and their application to any particular committee:

1. Does the committee reflect some concept of the "public interest" (however difficult it is to define that nebulous term), rather than the personal economic, political, or sectional interests of its chairman and members?

2. Are its criticisms constructive rather than destructive?

3. Does the committee emphasize fairly broad policy considerations, rather than minute details, and does it exercise restraint in substituting its judgment for that of the responsible administrative officials?

4. Does the committee use its great power for influencing public opinion responsibly, sticking to demonstrable facts and presenting them honestly and fairly, but at the same time searching out the full facts with thoroughness and vigor?

5. Does the committee stay within the limits of its mission?

6. Are its methods of operation fair to those who come under its scrutiny?

It should be clear from these criteria that responsibility—as applied to a committee—is not defined as formal accountability. Rather the term is intended to mean an awareness of the consequences of the use of power, a sensitivity to its effects; self-discipline and self-restraint exercised in terms of *responsibility* to the moral demands of a democratic political system.

This is a study of what, by these criteria, must stand as one of the most responsible major Congressional investigating committees—the Senate Special Committee to Investigate the National Defense Program, popularly known as the "Truman Committee" after its first chairman, Senator Harry S Truman.

It is not inappropriate that this committee should have been a wartime committee, for many of our more notorious investigating committees have functioned in periods of war or international crisis—especially the "cold war." The public passions, the clearly identified enemy, and the expansion of governmental activities at such times have all provided excuses for irresponsibility in investigating committees. The ability of the Truman Committee to oversee the war effort and at the same time to contribute to public understanding and support of that effort makes it a worthy subject for examination of a responsible committee in action.

There was nothing new in the creation of Congressional committees of investigation during wartime. Except for the Spanish-American War, according to Louis Smith, "such bodies have been created to investigate and criticize major aspects of the conduct of every war in which the United States has been engaged." [6] And during the war with Spain President McKinley forestalled an investigation by appointing his own commission to perform the same function.

Perhaps the most notorious of the war investigating committees was the Joint Committee on the Conduct of the War, which included in its sphere of investigation everything connected with the conduct of the Civil War. It insisted on not merely investigating and advising but on controlling the direction of the war. It attempted to gain control of Lincoln's Cabinet and to a very considerable extent did obtain control of the Army by driving out those officers to whom it had objections. One student comments:

The work of this committee, with its undocumented insinuations, loud publicity against the reputations of men who were not permitted to defend themselves, its suppression of testimony which did not support the official thesis about the war, its star chamber atmosphere, and its general disregard of the rules of fair procedure give it a distinct kinship with the Committee on Un-American Activities of a more recent age.[7]

The most objectionable activity of the Committee was its constant interference with military strategy and tactics. In particular it kept pushing for more vigorous action, with or without adequate preparation. It weakened Lincoln's control of his Administration throughout the war. The record of the Committee on the Conduct of the War had some influence on the Truman Committee. There was a clear desire, both among Committee members and others, that the Committee not use its great power in a manner that would interfere with the war as the Civil War Committee had.

Before Pearl Harbor, Congressional discontent with President Roosevelt's diplomacy found an outlet in a proposal by Senator Arthur H. Vandenberg to create a joint Senate-House committee on the conduct of national defense. The resolution was defeated with the clear understanding, in Smith's words, that "for the time being the Democratic majority in the Senate was prepared to leave defense administration and military control in the hands of the constitutional chief executive and commander-in-chief." [8] Shortly after the beginning of the war a resolution introduced by Senator Maloney to create a joint committee on war problems was likewise rejected. Nor was a joint committee to conduct a general investigation of the war effort established thereafter.

But there was no dearth of Congressional investigation of World War II. A Joint Committee on the Investigation of the Pearl Harbor Attack was established in September, 1945. This was the eighth investigation of that unhappy event, although it was the first to be conducted by Congress. The Truman Committee—officially the Senate Special Committee to Investigate the National Defense Program—was created on March 1, 1941, and published its final report on April 28, 1948. In the intervening seven years it conducted investigations on almost all phases of the war effort except those matters having to do with military strategy and tactics. In April, 1940, the House of Representatives established a Select Committee to Investigate Defense Migration, headed by Representative John H. Tolan. Popularly known as the Tolan Committee, this group investigated a much wider range of activities than its title would lead one to expect. It was the House equivalent of the Truman Committee, although its investigations did not range as widely and it tended to leave military matters to the Military Affairs Committee. In the three years of its existence it published thirty-four volumes of hearings and a number of reports covering all sorts of issues, including manpower and labor, health and welfare, and housing problems. Like the Truman Committee, it was very critical of the lack of centralized control over the mobilization program.

There were two other committees of great importance. Each house throughout the war period had a Select Committee on Small Business which held extensive hearings and issued numerous reports on the impact of defense and war policies, particularly contract distribution, on the smaller businesses of the nation. The House committee, under Wright Patman, issued nine volumes of hearings and six major reports on various aspects of the small business problem. The Senate committee, led by James E. Murray, issued ninety-nine volumes of hearings and a series of reports covering a variety of topics. A number of other special committees were set up in both houses of Congress to investigate some phase of the war effort. In general these committees dealt with relatively narrow segments of the war program.

Mention must also be made of the four military committees

in each house. They were the Military Affairs Committee, Naval Affairs Committee, Military Subcommittee of the Appropriations Committee, and Naval Subcommittee of the Appropriations Committee—*in each house.* This has since been reduced to two committees in each house, the Armed Services Committee and the Subcommittee on Armed Services Appropriations.

In the Senate the coordination between the Truman Committee and the other committees was relatively effective, particularly with the two military (as distinguished from naval) committees. Except for matters falling directly within the province of some existing committee, the Truman Committee handled almost all complaints and investigations relating to the war effort. Furthermore, Truman was a member of the Senate Military Affairs Committee and of the Subcommittee on Military Appropriations, and other members of the Committee also served on one or more of the committees concerned with military and naval affairs. The Appropriations Committee of the Senate conducted few investigations during the war. This was also true of the Senate Naval Affairs Committee, which had no standing subcommittees. The Military Affairs Committee, however, maintained several standing subcommittees throughout the war and conducted a number of special investigations of specific problems as they arose. It published hearings and reports on manpower, labor shortages, scientific and technological mobilization, Japanese relocation centers, the Alcan Highway, cartels, and reconversion, among other subjects.

Like its Senate counterpart, the House Committee on Appropriations was kept so busy handling the enormous volume of wartime appropriations business that it spent little time and effort in making investigations. Both the House Naval Affairs Committee and the House Military Affairs Committee undertook rather extensive investigations of some broad problems and of a number of specific, narrow issues relating to the war effort. The published hearings and reports of both these committees run to many volumes.

The great number of investigations of varying scope and duration covering most aspects of the war effort makes World War II the most investigated war in our history. The Truman Committee, however, was the only committee to make a systematic effort to survey the entire war program on a continuing basis. Its enabling resolution gave it virtually unlimited authority to examine and investigate all phases, both military and civilian, of the tremendous undertaking of mobilizing the nation and fighting the war.

The Committee's major interest was with the domestic side of the war effort—the industrial mobilization. But the military was also vitally interested in industrial mobilization. Throughout the war the armed services clashed with civilian agencies over mobilization policies, and the role of the military in industrial mobilization was itself an important issue. Consequently the Truman Committee came into frequent contact with the defense establishment throughout the war over a broad range of issues. Usually the Committee supported the civilian agencies, and an important part of its efforts was directed toward maintaining the dominance of the civilian agencies over the military with respect to the mobilization effort.

The Truman Committee's activities were broad enough and its operation dealt with sufficiently "touchy" issues so that its experience should enable us to draw some useful conclusions about the methods of operation of responsible Congressional investigating committees.

The chapters which follow deal with the creation, personnel, and procedures of the Committee, and with a number of case histories of particular investigations undertaken by the Committee. The conclusions are based on these case histories and on a general summary of the Committee's work.

1)   The Committee and Its Staff

In my opinion, the power of investigation is one of the most important powers of the Congress. The manner in which that power is exercised will largely determine the position and prestige of the Congress in the future.

Harry Truman [1]

THE COMMITTEE IS APPROVED

In January of 1941, after Senator Truman had rested from his arduous election campaign of 1940, he turned his attention to an accumulation of letters he was receiving from constituents in Missouri about waste and favoritism in the construction of Fort Leonard Wood. As a member of the Military Subcommittee of the Senate Appropriations Committee, he had already visited a number of Army camps in various places in the United States and was aware that waste seemed to be characteristic of the camp construction program then getting under way. Investigation convinced him that there was a tremendous waste of funds in the program and, besides, that war contracts were being concentrated in relatively few areas of the country and in relatively few companies.[2]

While Truman was working on a speech "on heading scandals

off before they started," William Helm, a reporter friend, suggested that he introduce a resolution to investigate the matter.[3] Truman delivered the speech to the Senate on February 10, 1941, and announced his intention of introducing a resolution asking for an investigation. In the speech he expressed more concern with possibilities for graft and the concentration of contracts than with waste. He began by saying:

There seems to be a policy in the national-defense set-up to concentrate all contracts and nearly all manufacturing that has to do with the national defense in a very small area. . . . The little manufacturer, the little contractor, and the little machine shop have been left entirely out in the cold. The policy seems to be to make the big man bigger and to put the little man completely out of business. . . .

I am reliably informed that from 70 to 90 per cent of the contracts let have been concentrated in an area smaller than England.

He concluded:

I am merely stating what I believe to be conditions that deserve investigation. If nothing is wrong, there will be no harm done. If something is wrong, it ought to be brought to light.[4]

The resolution (S. Res. 71) was introduced on February 13 and was referred to the Committee on Military Affairs. Truman already had the approval of Senator Robert R. Reynolds, the chairman of that Committee, and it issued a unanimous report in support of the resolution on February 22. It was then referred to the Senate Committee to Audit and Control the Contingent Expenses of the Senate, of which James F. Byrnes was chairman.

Byrnes held up the resolution. He was at that time very close to the President (he was appointed to the Supreme Court in June), and there was no enthusiasm in the Administration for an inquiry which might in any way resemble those of the Committee on the Conduct of the War. Perhaps Roosevelt feared political reprisals, for he had been very cool toward Truman during the Senator's uphill fight for re-election a few months before. Helm asked the President at a press conference what he thought of the idea, and Jonathan Daniels reports that "Roosevelt said he favored the investigation and hoped it would be thorough." [5] Daniels also reports that Roosevelt later said he approved of Truman as chairman of the committee.[6] These public statements, however, are not necessarily inconsistent with Byrnes's holding up the resolution on behalf of the Administration until a compelling reason for approving it appeared. At any rate, Truman later told Daniels, "I couldn't get Jimmy Byrnes to act. Everybody thought I wanted to set up a headline business like the Dies Committee. . . . After much haggling and delay he recommended that I be given the magnificent sum of $15,000 with which I started the activities of that committee." [7]

Apparently what changed Byrnes's mind was the threat of another investigation, headed by Representative E. Eugene Cox of Georgia, an implacable foe of the President.[8] Cox was making speeches about the defense program, stressing strikes and labor disputes. On January 13 he introduced a resolution to create a joint committee "to investigate and keep itself currently informed on all activities of the Federal Government in connection with the national defense." [9] On February 28 he introduced another resolution for a House investigation.

Samuel Lubell reports that Byrnes told Roosevelt, "I can fix that by putting the investigation into friendly hands," [10] for he was able to move faster than the House rules permitted. He asked Truman what he would do if his resolution were reported out.

According to Lubell, Truman replied: "I know there isn't a chance in the world of your reporting it out. But if you did I wouldn't conduct the investigation in a way that would hurt defense. You could count on me for that." [11]

Accordingly, Senate Resolution 71 was reported out on March 1, 1941, and adopted without objection from any of the sixteen Senators on the floor.[12] Byrnes made two alterations in the resolution. The number of members was increased from five to seven, and the ceiling on expenditures was reduced from Truman's requested $25,000 to $15,000.

The resolution granted extremely broad powers to the Committee. It was authorized and directed to make a full and complete study of the national defense program, including:

1. the types and terms of contracts awarded;
2. the methods by which contracts are awarded and contractors selected;
3. the utilization of small businesses;
4. the geographic distribution of contracts and the location of plants and facilities;
5. the effect of the defense program on labor and the migration of labor;
6. the performance of contracts and the accountings required of contractors;
7. benefits accruing to contractors with respect to amortization for the purposes of taxation or otherwise;
8. practices of management or labor, and prices, fees, and charges, which interfere with or unduly increase the costs of the program;
9. such other matters as the committee deems appropriate.[13]

The Committee was directed to report its findings and recommendations to the Senate, but it was not authorized to consider legislation and report out bills. It was given the usual powers to subpoena witnesses and documents and to hold hearings, administer oaths, and employ the necessary assistants.

Twice during its life the Committee received additional authority to conduct specific investigations. In May of 1941 the scope of its powers was broadened to include inquiries into the location of defense plants, and in October of 1942 the gas-rationing program was included.[14] These resolutions were really instructions to the Committee to investigate, rather than grants of authority, which were unnecessary. In July, 1946, the President signed an executive order giving the Committee authority to examine Federal income tax returns, providing aid in investigating the financial affairs of individuals and companies.

The Committee was continued through the 78th and 79th Congresses, with periodic increases in the limit of its expenditures. The requests for funds to continue the Committee's work were sometimes made at the time of the presentation to the Senate of an important report. Truman told Daniels, "After the Committee became known I always asked the Senate as a whole for expense money and the Committee on Audit and Control had to approve it." [15]

In January, 1947, the Senate of the 80th Congress authorized the continuance of the Committee for one year, but limited its scope to investigation of "excessive profits, fraud, corruption, waste, extravagance, mismanagement, incompetence, and inefficiency in expenditures, connected with World War II," and to transactions occurring within the United States and territories prior to June 30, 1946.[16] A number of extensions were permitted for the Committee to file reports, and it passed out of existence on June 11, 1948. Its records and remaining functions, as well as some members of its staff, were transferred to the permanent Investigation Subcommittee of the Committee on Expenditures in the Executive Department, later renamed the Committee on Government Operations.

THE CHAIRMAN

In March, 1941, when he became chairman of the Senate Special Committee to Investigate the Defense Program, Harry S Truman was virtually unknown outside of Washington and the state of Missouri. He was fifty-seven years old at the time. He had been elected to a second term in the Senate in 1940 after two opponents had split a majority of the primary votes to enable him to win the Democratic nomination. Raised in a small town (Independence, Missouri), he had had a long political career with the organization of Thomas J. Pendergast, where his unquestioned personal honesty made him a kind of "white knight" on display. His first term in the Senate had been marked by fairly regular but not undeviating support of the Administration, which regarded him as something of a liability because of his Pendergast affiliations. He had done little of note in his first term beyond serving an apprenticeship in Congressional investigation under the tutelage of Burton K. Wheeler during a long but unspectacular inquiry into railway finance.

He had the thirst for knowledge (particularly history) that sometimes characterizes a man with limited formal education. He maintained a near reverence for facts, which led him to make a cliché out of "get the facts and you can't go wrong" and sometimes to assume that genuine conflicts of interest would be resolved if the facts were available. But he brought to the Committee's work an intelligence capable of grasping the facts of the war effort, a persistence in seeking them, and the courage to follow them where they led.

Senator Truman's knowledge of history made him aware of the shortcomings of past investigations and supported his determination to avoid them. He was popular with his colleagues in the Senate. He cooperated fully with other Senators, making available to them full knowledge of the activities of his Committee, and frequently undertook investigations for them. He worked more conscientiously on the Committee's business than any other member and ruled "with a firm but not dictatorial hand." [17] But he had a modesty which enabled him to share the spotlight with other members. These qualities combined to make Truman a first-rate committee chairman.

Tom Connally, sixty-five in 1941, a Democrat from Marlin, Texas, was the senior member of the Committee. He was the most influential and powerful member of the Committee and the busiest—he was chairman of the Foreign Relations Committee and a ranking member of the important Judiciary and Finance Committees. Senator Connally was put on the Truman Committee to restrain the junior members and to provide some protection for the Administration. Although he tried to tone down some reports [18] and sometimes tried to protect administrative officials in the hearings, he also seems to have exerted considerable effort to protect the oil industry. He was one of the least active members in Committee affairs.

Carl A. Hatch replaced Carl Hayden before the Committee's work began and can therefore be considered an original member. He was a Democrat from Clovis, New Mexico. He was fifty-two. He was appointed to the Senate in 1933 and was re-elected to a full term in 1936. Usually a supporter of the Administration, he was best known for his sponsorship of the "Hatch Acts" aimed at corrupt political practices. Like Connally, he was a lawyer and an important member of the Judiciary Committee. He also was one of the less active members of the Truman Committee.

James M. Mead, a Democrat from Buffalo, New York, was fifty-five. He had started work for the Lackawanna Railroad at the age of twelve, had become a switchman, and was a life member of the Switchmen's Union of North America. He had served nineteen years in the House of Representatives when, in 1938, he was elected to fill an unexpired Senate term. He was re-elected to a full term in 1940. He was a loyal and regular Administration supporter and the member of the Committee who was most friendly toward organized labor. Although his populous state kept him busy with the affairs of constituents, he took an active interest in the Committee's business and became chairman upon Truman's resignation in 1944. After his failure to defeat Thomas E. Dewey for the governorship of New York in 1946, Mead was appointed to the Federal Power Commission by President Truman.

Mon C. Wallgren, a fifty-year-old Democrat from Everett, Washington, where he owned a retail optical and jewelry business, had served eight years in the House of Representatives and was both appointed and elected to the Senate in 1940. An active member, he was especially interested in problems affecting the lumber, light metals, and aircraft industries. He left the Senate to become Governor of Washington, and was appointed to the Federal Power Commission by President Truman in 1950.

Ralph Owen Brewster, from Dexter, Maine, was the Committee's senior Republican. Truman treated him as vice-chairman, and he took a very active part in the Committee's affairs. He was elected to the Senate in 1940 at the age of fifty-two. A lawyer, he was a relentless cross-examiner, but was the member most inclined to inject partisan political considerations into the Committee's deliberations. He became chairman during the 80th Congress, when the Committee lost much of its prestige.

Joseph H. Ball, at thirty-five the youngest member, was a Republican from Minnesota. He was appointed to the Senate in 1940 and elected to a full term in 1942. A Minneapolis newspaperman and political reporter, he was an outspoken internationalist when his state was still "isolationalist" and was somewhat independent in his political thinking (he supported Roosevelt in 1944). But he was generally conservative on domestic issues and was the most anti-labor member of the Committee; he clashed with both Sidney Hillman and John L. Lewis during hearings.

The ratio of five Democrats and two Republicans was apparently established to ensure maximum protection for the Administration. The fears seem to have been allayed at an early stage, however, for two Republicans and one Democrat were added to the Committee in October, 1941, when the Senate increased its membership to ten to enable it to carry a heavier work-load. Harley M. Kilgore was the Democrat and Clyde L. Herring and Styles Bridges were the Republicans. After only a few months Bridges was replaced by Harold H. Burton, and Homer Ferguson replaced Herring in January, 1943. Ferguson, Burton, and Kilgore were active members of the Committee, and all three, along with the original seven, were still serving on the Committee when Truman resigned the chairmanship in 1944.

Kilgore, forty-nine, was a Democrat from West Virginia. He was elected to the Senate in 1940. A small-town lawyer, his major interest on the Committee was in the organization of the mobilization effort, and, as chairman of the Committee's Subcommittee on Technological Mobilization, he endeavored to get centralized control of the defense effort. He was the most vigorous critic of the military on the Committee. For a brief period in 1946 he was the chairman.

Burton, a fifty-three-year-old Republican of Cleveland, Ohio, had been elected Senator in 1940. A lawyer, he had been active in the civic and political life of Cleveland. He was a moderate and internationalist Republican who was somewhat independent in his voting. In October, 1945, President Truman appointed him to the Supreme Court.

Ferguson, a Detroit Republican, was also fifty-three and a lawyer. He was elected to the Senate in 1942. An independent in local politics, he had served as a one-man grand jury and participated in an investigation of graft and corruption in Wayne County. He had taught law, practiced it, and served as a circuit judge. He was a vigorous cross-examiner and played an active role in the Truman Committee's work.

Some characteristics of the Committee members may be noted. All but Truman, Hatch, and Connally were serving their first terms, and neither Hatch nor Connally was a very active participant in the Committee's affairs. The other members did not have heavy responsibilities in their other committee assignments and were free to devote more of their energies to the work of the Truman Committee. Also, the Truman Committee offered them an opportunity to achieve public and Senatorial recognition more quickly than they could have in their standing committee assignments.

There was a wide geographical distribution of members. All had exhibited some degree of independence in politics. Except for Connally and Ball, all were in their fifties.

All except Mead were middle-class in social background. Mead came from a poor working-class family and had been an active union member, which accounts for his pro-labor views and his antipathy to big business. But he had been a successful politician for many years and had acquired middle-class values and attitudes. The others, with the possible exception of Burton, whose law practice involved some corporation work, were middle-class in the traditional pattern. Mostly from small towns, the businessmen among them were small-businessmen, the lawyers had small-businessmen for clients. They appear to epitomize middle-class values of their respective areas. This may account for their unanimity and the vigor of their criticism of the conduct of big business and its representatives in the government. Traditional values of patriotism and thrift conflicted, especially because this was wartime, with the greed and waste the Committee uncovered. The moral tone of the Committee's reports seems to reflect an American tendency to pose political issues in moral terms.

It is not surprising that the Committee had a high degree of homogeneity. Few Senators were anxious to become members of the Committee, and Truman had considerable freedom in choosing the members, except perhaps for Tom Connally, who was appointed as a restraining influence.

Two Washington observers described the distinguishing mark of the ten long-time members of the Truman Committee as "a sort of unspectacular competence." [19] But that sort of competence, plus a good staff, produced exceptional results.

THE STAFF

The caliber of the staff of an investigating committee is of prime importance. Even the most conscientious member of a particular committee has the great burden of work on other committees, the demands of his constituents, and the necessity of being at least vaguely familiar with the mass of complex legislation on which he must vote. He cannot possibly acquaint himself with all the detailed work involved in an extensive investigation. And when the committee covers as much ground and as many complex subjects as did the Truman Committee, the staff must make such decisions as which matters to investigate further and which to give up. Many investigations were abandoned by the Truman Committee as unfruitful or unwarranted on the basis of preliminary checks by the staff without consultation with committee members. Furthermore, when a committee conducts public hearings and issues reports, its members risk their reputations on the quality and thoroughness of the staff work.

The Truman Committee staff was headed by a very able chief counsel. Truman later told Jonathan Daniels, "I went to see Attorney General [Robert H.] Jackson and told him what I was going to do. If we find anything wrong I'll leave it to you to prosecute, but I want the best investigator you've got." [20] Jackson sent Hugh Fulton to see Truman. Fulton, a graduate of the University of Michigan Law School, was then thirty-five. He had already acquired a reputation as an effective United States

Attorney, with successful investigations and prosecutions of Howard C. Hopson of Associated Gas and Electric Company, a judge of the Federal Circuit Court of Appeals, an investment banker, and "several others in high positions who had strayed from the straight and narrow path." [21] Truman's first impression of Fulton was not very favorable: "He came in wearing a derby hat, a big fat fellow with a squeaky voice. I said to myself, 'Oh shucks!' However, I paid him more than half of the money I had, $8,500 a year which was $500 more than he was getting." [22] Fulton was assured that he would have no interference with his running of the committee staff and his conduct of committee business, and that he would not be subjected to political pressure. Although Fulton and Truman broke after the latter became President, Fulton said later that no pressure was exerted, either on him or on anyone else that he knew of, in the conduct of any investigation.[23] In his work Fulton set high standards, and he insisted that all other staff members meet them.

Truman and Fulton assembled a small staff. In August, 1941, the $15,000 limit on expenditures was increased, and the Committee thereafter was able to get all the funds it needed. The size of the staff and total expenditures were quite modest, however, considering the volume and scope of the work undertaken by the Committee. After the staff had settled into a routine it normally consisted of Fulton as chief counsel, an associate counsel, an assistant counsel, a chief investigator, 12 to 18 other investigators, a committee clerk, an editor, and about the same number of clerical personnel. Walter Hehmeyer, who served as an investigator, also handled press relations. Both the chairman and the chief counsel had executive assistants who also held other staff positions. The first associate counsel, Charles Patrick Clark, served as Truman's executive assistant, but after he left to join the Army Matthew Connelly, the chief investigator, took over this function. The chief counsel's executive assistant was usually the assistant counsel.[24]

Matthew Connelly, the chief investigator, had served as an investigator or staff member with a number of Congressional committees and was one of a group known in Washington as "committee dicks." He was politically astute and became President Truman's appointments secretary. He assembled the group of investigators, who received their training on the job. Most were young lawyers or accountants with little or no previous experience. One of them acknowledges that their youth and inexperience made them "pretty open" in their investigations.[25] This openness undoubtedly made it easier for the investigated to cover up.

The Committee also used investigators from other government agencies, although this practice was restricted after the summer of 1942 in accordance with a ruling of the Comptroller General. Rudolph Halley, who succeeded Fulton as chief counsel in September, 1944, came to the Committee in 1942 from the Anti-Trust Division of the Department of Justice, where he had worked on committee business.[26]

It is impossible to define exactly the line between staff and committee member functions. Fulton and Truman usually conferred daily. Both were early risers, and their conferences usually took place in the early morning. The Committee met once or twice a week in a room behind Truman's office known to intimates as "Harry's Doghouse." The meetings were attended by committee members, Fulton, other staff members working on the subjects under consideration, and sometimes by other government officials concerned. Donald M. Nelson, chairman of the War Production Board, was a frequent visitor to "Harry's Doghouse." Truman and Fulton together ran the Committee, Fulton supervising the detailed work but keeping Truman constantly informed.

THE ROLE OF THE COMMITTEE

The Truman Committee saw itself as a watchdog over the war effort, an agency for "digging out the facts." It assumed that scrutiny and exposure of incompetence, stupidity, administrative rigidity, cupidity, and dishonesty would result in correction, at least in the atmosphere of war. The Committee assumed that winning the war constituted a common goal which united most men in government and which could be relied upon to bring about the elimination of such conditions as the Committee might demonstrate were interfering with the war effort.

To some extent the assumption was valid. The position of anyone connected with the war program whose actions could be shown to be dictated by his personal interests was very difficult indeed. But the easy assumption that winning the war was the cherished goal of all exaggerated the degree to which self-seeking was abandoned during the war. The Truman Committee's records contain an impressive amount of evidence as to the prevalence of wartime self-seeking. And the assumption tended to overlook the degree to which there were honest and sincere differences as to how best to win the war.

In his first speech to the Senate on the subject, Truman stressed the watchdog role he expected the committee to perform. "I have had considerable experience in letting public contracts," he said, "and I have never yet found a contractor who, if not watched, would not leave the Government holding the bag. We are not doing him a favor if we do not watch him." [27]

Also, there seems to have been a general recognition that the 116 post-mortem investigations of World War I constituted an exercise in futility. Nothing very constructive came of those investigations and there was no reason to expect salutary results from another set to be conducted after World War II. Truman, in fact, hoped to avoid investigations after the war by conduct-

ing them as the war progressed. In this he was right, for the post-
war investigations of World War II were limited to those carried
on by wartime committees winding up their affairs, mostly by
the Truman Committee. The experience of the Committee un-
derlines this point. As its investigations turned toward the end
of the war to post-mortem examinations of cases involving corrupt and fraudulent activities, the quality of the investigations
and the decisiveness of its reports declined, reaching the nadir
in the investigation of the Hughes Aircraft Company in 1947,
as Howard Hughes and Senator Brewster traded accusations of
bribery and blackmail.

The Committee was acutely aware of the possibility of criticism that it was acting like the Lincoln era's Committee on the
Conduct of the War, and reference was frequently made in
reports and in speeches by members and staff to the Committee's
careful avoidance of matters of military strategy and tactics.
Truman had read the Library of Congress copy of the hearings
of the Civil War committee and is fond of quoting Robert E. Lee
to the effect that "that committee was worth two divisions" to
him.[28] As late as May, 1943, when the Committee's reputation
for responsibility and for confining its work to the domestic
aspects of the war effort were firmly established, it indicated its
sensitivity to the issue by beginning a report:

> The committee never have investigated, and they still believe that
> they should not investigate, military and naval strategy or tactics. . . .
> The committee have the utmost confidence in Admiral King, Chief
> of Operations of the Navy, and General Marshall, Chief of Staff of
> the Army, and we believe that matters of tactics and strategy should
> be left entirely in their hands.[29]

The issue came up immediately after Pearl Harbor. Both in
and out of Congress there were some, including the influential
New York Times, who doubted the value of investigation and
criticism while the war was in progress. The Committee held an

executive session in which the question of continuing was thoroughly discussed, and issued a definitive statement of policy on December 10, 1941:

The Committee held an executive session for the purpose of determining how they could best contribute to the defense of the Nation.

The Committee never have investigated, and they still believe that they should not investigate, military and naval strategy or tactics. Such matters should be handled strictly by the Military and Naval Affairs Committees of the Congress.

From their inception the Special Committee have concerned themselves with the nonmilitary aspects of the defense program, that is to say, with seeing to it that the defense articles which the Army and Navy have determined that they need are produced in a minimum of time at a minimum of cost and with as little disruption of the civilian economy as possible.

During the 8 months in which the Special Committee have operated, they have noted and called attention to many things which have adversely affected production, particularly the failure to increase the production of strategic materials soon enough and fast enough, and the failure to utilize in the defense program the existing facilities of the intermediate and small manufacturing establishments. By their action, the Special Committee believe that they have forced a greater attention to these problems; they believe that the various defense agencies are giving now more adequate attention to them; but they believe also that it is necessary to continue a constant watch for the purpose of assuring that such problems are met head-on and solved.

The Special Committee have no doubt of the ability of the United States to win this war. It is simply a question of when and at what cost the war will be won, but that is a most important question. The Committee are determined the war should not continue weeks or months longer because of the failure to get the production which we need as soon as possible. An unnecessary prolongation of war caused by failure to produce as fast, efficiently, and economically as possible would cause an unnecessary loss of life and property.[30]

The only time the Committee made any mention of a military matter not related to supply occurred in September, 1942, when

Truman, in the course of a personal report to the Senate on the Committee's activities, reluctantly brought up the subject of the unity of command, which neither the Military Affairs Committee nor the Naval Affairs Committee could handle because of their limited jurisdictions. He said:

As disclosed by the report of the Roberts committee, lack of unity of command was one of the most important circumstances contributing to the disaster at Pearl Harbor. Here again the public and the Congress have been assured that attention has been given to this problem and that unity of command has been achieved. But the confidential report to the Committee made by the Senators who recently made a 4,000 mile tour of all the important military points in Alaska indicates that more attention should be given immediately to obtaining a workable unity of command, particularly in Alaska.[31]

Truman later said of the Committee's role, "I just wanted to help the President win the war." [32] There was great opportunity to do so, without any necessity for going into strategy and tactics. For Roosevelt's preoccupation with the military and foreign aspects of the war, and his indifference to the domestic aspects, left a near vacuum to be filled. Nor did the restriction mean that the Committee's contacts with the military were negligible. The armed services were interested in virtually all problems of war mobilization, and the Committee clashed with them over a broad variety of issues.

The Truman Committee also tried to exercise considerable restraint with respect to the civilian agencies it dealt with. On a radio program in July, 1941, Truman stated the Committee's policy:

I would like to point out that the national-defense committee does not seek to substitute its judgment for that of other governmental departments or agencies of defense. They have their own jobs to do. However, we can and will and do ascertain the facts about what they are doing and why they are doing it. And we bring these facts to light and suggest that they consider changes or different courses of action whenever we think it necessary to the effective working of the defense program. We leave the determination up to them, but we want to be very certain that no stone is left unturned.[33]

And the First Annual Report repeated, "The Committee has not and does not intend to substitute its judgment on such matters for the judgment of the executive agencies involved." [34]

Such a degree of self-restraint on the part of an influential Congressional committee would be extraordinary indeed. And it must be said that the Truman Committee came closer to the ideal it set itself, especially in its dealings with WPB Chairman Nelson, than do most Congressional committees. On the other hand, we must recognize that an important objective of Congressional investigations is the influencing or controlling of policy of administrative agencies. The Truman Committee was no exception. As it gained prestige, power, and authority, its reports tended to emphasize less the presentation of facts and more the recommendation of courses of action to the executive agencies. The Committee quickly came to expect its views to be accorded respect and compliance.

Two examples of the changing tenor of the reports indicate the Committee's increasing concern with prompt action in response to Committee demands. In September, 1942, Truman reported to the Senate on the activities of the Committee, which had been doing much of its work in private for some months. In the course of the report he said:

Such waste must stop. . . . It is not sufficient for those in charge of construction to render lip service to the principles of economy enunciated by the Committee. To make real progress they must make examples of those contractors who permit waste and inefficiencies. . . .

This Committee called Mr. Nelson before it and promised him the utmost cooperation, stating that if anyone, even a Cabinet member, should hesitate to carry out Mr. Nelson's suggestions, this committee wanted to be informed about it. . . .

Mr. Nelson has agreed with the Committee's private recommendations that he get 'tough,' but the Committee wants to see results. . . . Mr. Nelson should show speed . . . and appoint a two-fisted, competent man to remedy the steel situation.

Weeks ago the Committee sent a confidential report on tank lighters to the Secretary of the Navy setting forth detailed facts and referring to Navy and Army reports which, in the opinion of the Committee, established that the Bureau of Ships should be subjected to severe censure for having failed adequately to provide the best tank lighters known to them. But the Committee did expect that in a matter of such importance the Secretary of the Navy would take prompt and effective action. I am sorry to say that so far as the Committee can ascertain, the Secretary of the Navy has not yet made up his mind what to do. The Committee will insist upon action by him.

This war must not be lost, and it need not be lost. But we must realize that it can be lost. The Committee will continue its investigations, and so far as possible, will do so privately. It will support every two-fisted fighter who tries to make progress, but it will insist that progress be made.[35]

And at the conclusion of the report on Conflicting War Programs, presented in May, 1943, the Committee commented:

Energetic, aggressive men, striving to meet war needs, will tend to clash when their duties bring them into conflict. But destructive, wasteful feuding must be suppressed.

The task of control and guidance is of utmost importance. Clear leadership in strong hands is required. The influence from above must be always towards unity. Where necessary, heads must be knocked together.[36]

In partial defense of the Committee's ventures into head-knocking, it may be noted that there was frequent need for it in wartime Washington; the President was reluctant and usually too busy with other matters to do it, and he had no other agency to do it for him until the Office of War Mobilization was established.

In short, although the Truman Committee conceived its role

to be that of a "watchdog" and an agency for "digging up the facts," its intimate involvement with all of the domestic aspects of the war program led it directly into the role of influencing policy in the mobilization agencies, including the military.

2)   Committee Procedures

We decided that we did not want to make it either a smear committee or a whitewash committee.

Joseph H. Ball [1]

"By general agreement," Bailey and Samuel say, "one of the most successful and responsible Congressional investigations of recent years was that conducted by the so-called 'Truman Committee.' " [2] A considerable measure of the Committee's effectiveness and the esteem in which it was generally held must be attributed to the way it conducted its business. Former Representative Jerry Voorhis has set forth some factors which determine the success of Congressional investigations, against which the Truman Committee may be judged:

The effectiveness of congressional investigations—as distinguished from the amount of publicity they receive—is dependent upon five principal factors. These are: the character and capabilities of the committee chairman; the care with which committee reports are prepared and the extent to which emphasis is placed on the official reports rather than interim statements by individual committee members; the calibre of the committee staff; the degree to which fair and judicious rules of procedure are adopted and observed; and the absence of partisan or political bias.[3]

The calibre of the chairman and the committee staff, particularly the chief counsel, have been discussed. This chapter is devoted to procedures followed by the Committee in its work.

RELATIONS WITH GOVERNMENT AGENCIES

The Truman Committee's relations with the Senate were excellent. Truman kept the Senate informed of the Committee's activities. Other Senators were welcome at its hearings and were frequently permitted to ask questions of witnesses, subject to the control of the chairman. For example, in its investigation of the Army hotel acquisition program, Senator Claude D. Pepper of Florida was permitted to take an active part, both in developing the case before public hearings were held and during the hearings themselves. Consequently, many Senators passed on complaining letters from constituents to the Committee for investigation. Truman said later, "It got so Senators would ask me, 'Harry, won't you investigate this for me?' " [4]

The most important source of potential friction within the Senate was the Military Affairs Committee. Little or no friction developed, however, because its chairman, Senator Robert R. Reynolds, had given his approval to Truman before the latter introduced the resolution to set up the Committee. The absence of friction was also due to the practice of the Committee to defer to the Military Affairs Committee in matters in which the latter had a clear or stated interest. The Committee sometimes deferred to other Congressional committees with a special interest in some phase of the war effort. As a result there were a few issues, such as price control, which escaped its scrutiny.

Furthermore, the Committee members had interlocking memberships on other committees of the Senate. This web of memberships strengthened the Truman Committee's position with other committees and facilitated its coverage of such a broad and complex subject as mobilization. Three of its members—

Truman, Kilgore, and Wallgren—were members of the Military Affairs Committee. Two—Truman and Mead—were on the Appropriations Committee, and Truman was a member of its Military Subcommittee. Mead was on the Small Business Committee, and Brewster was on the Naval Affairs Committee. In addition the Committee had contacts with the Committees on Foreign Affairs (Connally), Education and Labor (Ball), and Judiciary (Burton and Hatch). Also, of course, each member had a number of other, less important committee assignments.

Truman says he kept the members of his committee interested and active by "giving them responsibility and keeping them informed." [5] He early established a number of two- or three-man subcommittees. Reports to the Senate were made by the full Committee, but a report originally prepared by a subcommittee was usually presented to the Senate by the subcommittee's chairman. There is no record of anyone's objecting to the publicity thus received. Also, in the public hearings Truman was solicitous of the interests of the other members and gave them ample opportunity to make points and develop testimony; for example:

> *Mr. [Marriner S.] Eccles.*   I didn't come up here at my own request. I knew nothing about what I was coming for.
> *The Chairman.*   You came at the request of Senator Mead, who wanted to ask you that question, and he did. We thank you for coming and I appreciate very much the information you have given us.[6]

The Committee had liaison officers assigned to it—at Truman's request—in the War Department, the Navy Department, the War Production Board, the Maritime Commission, and the War Shipping Administration. In addition, the Committee had, as a regular member of its staff, Brigadier General Frank E. Lowe. He was selected by General George C. Marshall as one in whom Marshall had confidence, but his sole function was to serve the Committee, and his contacts with the Army were usually through its liaison officer.

Army liaison with Congress was handled rather loosely in the early defense period. On May 8, 1941, Julius H. Amberg was named Special Assistant to the Secretary of War to handle war frauds, Congressional liaison, liaison with the War Production Board, and other miscellaneous duties with a legal flavor. Lieutenant Colonel Arthur R. Wilson was made liaison officer to the Truman Committee. On March 8, 1942, a Legislative and Liaison Division was formed under Major General Wilton B. Persons in the office of the Judge Advocate General. In April, 1943, Amberg was put under Persons but continued to handle a variety of special matters for the Secretary of War very much as he had before.[7] Between December 6, 1941 and October 16, 1945, Miles H. Knowles, a lawyer, served as a member of Amberg's staff in charge of Congressional investigations. There was a directive to all units to channel all Congressional inquiries through him, which, although breached on a number of occasions, was fairly well kept. He would get the information to answer complaints, prepare a report, and send it up to Capitol Hill. Knowles has said that usually the officers concerned wanted to look over his replies before they were sent to Congress, but he sent them as *his* reports. He found that he was more willing to admit mistakes than the Army; the Army was seldom willing to admit its mistakes.[8] The Committee found that in both services the civilian personnel assigned to liaison work were much more cooperative than the career officers.

The Navy's liaison with Congress was less formal than the Army's. Some of it, for a time, was handled by an assistant in the Office of the Secretary of the Navy named Adlai E. Stevenson. The Truman Committee's official contact was a Captain John Kennedy, assigned to the Office of the Chief of Naval Operations. Some Congressional liaison work was carried on by the Navy at the bureau level, for example by Frank Nash in the Bureau of Ships.[9] Still, the Navy in general seemed more skillful in its relations with the Committee than the Army. The Navy usually gave the appearance of cooperation, even while covering up, and was able to mislead committee investigators. The intransigence of Army officers made it easier for the staff to track down what was wanted.[10]

Liaison with the other agencies mentioned was a rather simple matter; the liaison officer served as a contact from whom the Committee could get information when it was desired. However, Committee relations with the War Production Board deserve special mention, for they were exceptionally good and must be counted as contributing to whatever success is credited the WPB. Nelson met frequently with the Committee and even more often with Truman. And his liaison man, Edwin A. Locke, Jr., kept the Committee constantly informed as to what was going on in the WPB. When the WPB ran into difficulty, Locke would "leak" the news to the Truman Committee, which then would proceed to take action or exert pressure. This was particularly true in the cases of WPB-military conflicts, in which the Committee usually sided with the WPB.[11]

Relations with one other agency deserve comment. The Department of Justice was, of course, responsible for prosecuting violations of law turned up by the Truman Committee. The Department's War Frauds Unit was given full access to Committee files and was given any required assistance by the Committee staff. But the Committee's relations with the Anti-Trust Division were probably more important. Thurman W. Arnold and Wendell Berge of the Division were forced to hold up all anti-trust suits for the duration of the war. The Army forced a consent decree on the Division in the Standard Oil case, whereupon Arnold went to the Truman Committee and put the story on the public record. Thereafter the Anti-Trust Division, handi-

capped in its efforts to administer the anti-trust laws of the
country, found the threat of exposure before the Truman Committee an extremely uesful device in securing compliance with
the law.[12]

HANDLING INVESTIGATIONS [13]

Many of the Committee's investigations were undertaken on its
own initiative, either on the basis of continuing concern with an
issue such as renegotiation or because of problems in the press,
as in the case of the soft coal strike of 1941 or the investigation of conflicting war programs in 1943. It also received, of
course, tips from government officials who went to it for aid.
But, particularly after the Committee achieved prestige and
fame, it received thousands of letters from private citizens giving
"tips" about various aspects of the war effort. The investigation of fraudulent inspection at Carnegie-Illinois Steel was the
result of a tip from a disillusioned employee. Truman received
"two or three thousand letters from individual farmers" concerning their inability to get farm machinery, leading to an investigation of this subject.[14] The bulk of the complaints reached
the Committee from private citizens—mostly by mail, although
a few came in person or telephoned. People wrote that some
project in their community was being handled wastefully or that
they were being paid for "standing around doing nothing" by
some war contractor on a cost-plus contract. They wrote if they
saw projects whose immediate objectives were not obvious to
them. The Committee received a great many letters, for example, about the Manhattan Project. Truman went to Henry L.
Stimson and was told that it was an undertaking paralleling a
German project and that the first country to succeed would
probably win the war. Truman dropped the matter there.[15]

The Committee received many letters from people with ideas
for winning the war or solving some troublesome problem. If

the idea seemed to have any merit it was called to the attention of the responsible officials. Where officialdom had neglected some promising idea, pressure was brought to bear for reconsideration. The Committee was quite critical of the Navy, for example, for giving the helicopter only passing consideration. And it helped get attention for an individual who had devised a rough means of firing a rocket projectile.

The Committee's mail also carried the usual complement of "crackpot" ideas. "One proposal advocated that every soldier in our army be supplied with a single-seater airplane into which would be shoveled a 'few square yards of good American soil.' This vast armada would then take off, fly over Tokyo, dump the earth and thus bury Japan in defeat." Another suggestion was to build a few huge steel spheres with great spikes which would roll along "chewing up armies and cities like a meat grinder. Just two of them could stop the war in no time." [16]

The complaints were assigned to an investigator by the counsel or chief investigator, and the investigator proceeded to make a preliminary investigation to determine whether the complaint had any merit and whether the Committee had jurisdiction. If further action was called for, the investigator continued to uncover the facts. Since the staff tended to specialize, they usually developed contacts who could be depended upon for accurate information in those agencies with no liaison. These informal contacts were extremely important, for they provided a constant source of reliable information. Thus, the need for tips from agencies where such contacts were established was minimized. The investigator developed the facts in the case from these contacts, from the author of the complaint, and from other agencies of the government which might have the information, such as the Budget Bureau, the Justice Department, or the General Accounting Office. Sometimes field investigations were required. If it was necessary to examine files this was done by request if possible, by subpoena when cooperation was not forthcoming. But the staff tried to secure cooperation if at all possible. There were no dramatic staff raids on any one's files, as there have been in some investigating committees since the war.

The investigator would then submit a report summarizing the facts without conclusions, although he might make recommendations as to further action. The charges were still regarded as allegations. This report was then considered by one of the counsel. If it was a minor matter, a final decision was usually made by the chief counsel. Decisions in important matters were made by the chairman, after informal discussion with Committee members or after an executive session. If there was no need for further information the investigation was closed. If further action was needed the case was taken up by the full Committee or assigned to one of the subcommittees. Most cases were handled by the full Committee, although the subcommittees were responsible for some of the most important issues.

This account suggests that staff members spent all their time running down "tips." In this respect it is misleading. The Committee had a basic planned program with respect to the major continuing problems of the war effort. Each staff investigator tended to become a specialist in one or two of these problems. In addition he would be assigned complaints or tips to check, including those which related to his special fields of interest. Many of the letters were merely turned over to the appropriate agency of the government for a brief report for the Committee to use in answering the letter. A large accumulation of letters on one subject usually brought at least a thorough investigation by the staff, and some important investigations began in the manner described. The flood of complaints and tips probably diverted some of the Committee's energies that might better have been devoted to problems of policy and administration into a hunt for fraud and corruption. Also, there was doubtless some

fragmentation of the Committee's efforts as a result of its conscientious handling of complaints and tips. On the other hand,
the Committee did maintain its planned coverage of the major
issues of policy and administration, although it did not cover
some issues, such as price control, which were pre-empted by
other committees. Most of the time the staff was able to do both
jobs. And there was certainly some value in having a committee
with public prestige handle these complaints. The writers who
complained without justification may have been mollified by the
Truman Committee's assurance that everything was all right.
And many minor matters were corrected because the Committee
passed on a complaint to the offending agency.

There seem to have been no clear-cut criteria for deciding
which investigations to follow up once it was determined that
there was a justification for Committee action. Fulton and the
Committee apparently assigned priorities on the basis of such
factors as the urgency of investigations already under way, the
other obligations of members, political factors which might be
involved, the effort required to carry an investigation through,
and whether or not other Congressional committees were studying the problem. In general, major issues of the war effort received a higher priority than cases of fraud or corruption, and
some of the latter were passed by because of the pressure of
more important business.

When an issue was turned over to it, the full Committee or a
subcommittee might hold conferences with the parties concerned, undertake further investigation, or hold public or executive hearings. Public hearings were held unless security considerations dictated otherwise. Although the Committee objected
if it thought the Army or Navy was unnecessarily secretive, it
did not make hearings or reports public if the services thought
they would in any way endanger the national security.

The responsibility for preparing for the hearings rested with the chief counsel. He had to notify (or subpoena) the witnesses, who were either those who knew the facts of a case or those responsible in the situation. The system of liaison resulted in an orderly procedure for calling subordinate officers in at least the major agencies and the armed services. But the Committee did not try to hold a subordinate responsible when the responsibility properly rested with a superior; it insisted on calling the responsible officer before it.

The chief counsel also had responsibility for scheduling hearings—in consultation with the chairman and members—and for informing members of the facts and issues in the case at hand. Much of this was done in the course of his regular consultation with them, but Fulton also prepared memoranda setting down the pertinent facts and chronologies or briefs listing the important questions to be covered. The following is a brief pertaining to an appearance of Donald M. Nelson on the subject of dollar-a-year men:

1. In discussing dollar-a-year and w.o.c. men, Mr. Nelson will probably state that it is necessary to secure such men, since they are experts in their field. He should be asked why, conceding this to be so, these men do not disassociate themselves from their business connections upon being employed by the Government, and why they do not work for the Government on a Government salary. He will probably reply that such men will not come to work for the Government if this were the case, because they cannot afford to live on a Government salary. Mr. Nelson should then be asked as to whether he himself severed, very recently, all connections with his former employers, after his appointment as Chairman of the War Production Board. Mr. Nelson will undoubtedly answer in the affirmative. He should then be asked why other dollar-a-year men do not see fit to follow his example. Then, too, Mr. Nelson could be asked why he found it necessary to sever all private connection. If he states that the immensity of his job and the exigencies of his present Government position required this disestablishment from his former employment, the question is raised as to why these same principles do not apply to

every dollar-a-year and w.o.c. man employed in the Federal Government.

In response to Mr. Nelson's argument that these men would not serve in the Government if forced to relinquish their private salaries, the testimony should indicate that in this hour of emergency every person must place himself at the service of the Government without thought of personal aggrandizement. If men are being drafted for $21.00 per month to serve in the Army, there is a serious reflection on the patriotism of a person who refuses to work for the Government for a salary ranging from $5000 to $10,000 per year.

2. The questioning might bring out that these dollar-a-year men not only continue to receive their salaries from their firms, but in addition receive a Government reimbursement of $10.00 per day, so that financially speaking, they gain instead of lose. The point might be raised that they are making sacrifices inasmuch as their firms are not receiving the benefit of their counsel, and that as a result the efficiency of the firm is impaired. In this connection it might be noted that in the usual instance, firms that dollar-a-year men are connected with, have not suffered as a result of these men volunteering their services, but rather have enjoyed very sizeable increases in business as a result of defense contracts. Furthermore, it is hard to concede that these men are making any kind of sacrifice personally, since they enjoy their former income, as well as an augmented income by way of Government reimbursement. A true sacrifice would be their resigning all private connections and devoting themselves 100% to Government work at a Government salary. Certainly soldiers drafted in the Army are making great sacrifices in having to relinquish their jobs and be in the Army for $21.00 per month.

3. These dollar-a-year and w.o.c. men have consistently maintained that business cannot go on as usual, that we all must make sacrifices. The testimony should indicate that this does not apply in the case of these men who have enunciated this "sacrifice is necessary" policy.

4. The questioning should indicate just why these firms are willing to pay these men their full salaries while they are employed for the Government. Do these large firms pay the full salaries of the men employed by them who have been drafted in the Army? The answer is obvious.

5. If these dollar-a-year and w.o.c. men do not render their corporation any service, then have the corporations received permission from the stockholders to pay these sums of money without any commensurate services being rendered? Are not these payments really in the nature of gifts by the corporations? But these corporations do not give gifts without any hope of return.[17]

The chief counsel also notified members and witnesses as to when and where they were to appear. The witnesses were normally notified a few days in advance, but not always, and occasionally there were complaints from witnesses that insufficient notice had been given. The witnesses were not informed in detail as to the subject of the investigation. This sometimes caused unnecessary lack of preparation on the part of witnesses, in addition to the deliberate unpreparedness resulting from a desire to evade the Committee's questions.

If the hearing was public an announcement was made as to time, place, subject, and witnesses. The press was usually briefed in advance on the subject matter to be covered and the witnesses to be called.

The witness was generally given an opportunity to read a prepared statement if he wished to do so, although he was subject to interruptions and questions. Occasionally a summary of the statement was presented orally with the full text submitted for the record. Although the statement by the witness frequently consumed valuable time without much contribution to the Committee's work and was occasionally used for purposes of delay, it was an important protection to the witness, allowing him to get his story before the Committee and the public at the beginning of the hearing.

Usually he was then questioned by Fulton or one of the other counsel to develop the facts in the case as quickly as possible. Two Washington reporters have described Fulton's conduct of a hearing:

In his method of conducting a hearing, Fulton also varied from the conventional pattern. He never tried to entrap or bully a witness, or to overdramatize a line of questioning purely for the sake of headlines. He brought into each session a carefully prepared list of questions, designed to lead the witness into the heart of his story with a minimum of lost motion. The questioning itself often was done by the chairman or the Senator with a special interest in the subject at issue.[18]

The questioning continued by counsel and members until the conclusion of the hearing. Non-member Senators were frequently permitted to question witnesses, and occasionally Representatives or other government officials were permitted to do so. While there are obvious dangers in this practice, a firm and responsible chairman can prevent a non-member's taking over the show—and Truman did so. Witnesses were not generally permitted to ask questions of each other, although the chairman accepted questions from one witness to another on a few occasions.

The Committee was scrupulous in its efforts to avoid functioning as a court. It attempted to leave determination as to guilt or innocence of law-breaking to the Department of Justice and the courts and to confine its determinations to fact-finding. Nevertheless, the individual witness was given most of the protections that he would have had in court. He was permitted counsel, to whom he could refer questions for assistance, although cross-examination was not permitted. He was permitted to consult his attorney for explanation of points and advice, and the attorney was permitted to make objections to the line of questioning.

Two other rights were accorded individual witnesses. The witness was permitted to introduce documents into the record to support his case. And the Committee accepted the use of the Fifth Amendment, refraining from attempts to draw conclusions from its use. To ensure the accuracy of its transcripts, galley proofs of the testimony were sent to all witnesses for corrections, although substantial changes in testimony were not permitted.

In spite of the privileges accorded witnesses, which resemble the rights of the courtroom, the Truman Committee's hearings were not generally conducted on the courtroom model. Those involving broad issues of public policy with government officials as witnesses were rarely conducted in that manner. There was a tendency for hearings involving cases of fraud and corruption to develop in a manner somewhat akin to the courtroom trial, in spite of the intention of the Committee not to have them do so. In part this was a result of the subject of investigation, in part a result of the fact that some of the witnesses were antagonistic to the Committee.

The courtroom model is inappropriate for a Congressional committee to follow, for a committee is not a court. By its very nature, the committee hearing forces the individual to be a witness against himself. Therefore, it would have been more appropriate for the War Frauds Unit of the Justice Department to have handled all cases of war frauds and corruption. On the other hand, these cases involved contracts with the government in which Congress had a legitimate interest. In such cases the privileges accorded witnesses before the Truman Committee provided an important protection to them. But the ultimate protection depends upon the restraint of committees in refraining from inquiring into personal matters in which there is not a clear and legitimate public interest. The Truman Committee made a sincere effort to keep its investigations of fraud and corruption directed at conditions rather than individuals, and achieved a considerable measure of success.

The Truman Committee's code of procedure was worked out by Truman and Fulton. Although it was not written down, it was consistently followed, at least during the period when Truman was chairman and Fulton was chief counsel.

The conduct of the Committee members was not always exemplary, although a high standard of conduct characterized the Committee's hearings and the departures were clearly exceptions. Members sometimes injected irrelevant matters into the discussion and occasionally tried to protect witnesses from legitimate lines of questioning. Senator Connally was sometimes prone to protect high officials of the Administration. High feeling was also exhibited on occasion, as in this exchange with John L. Lewis:

Senator Ball.   Mr. Lewis, you are not seriously trying to tell the committee that any large number of workers in the United States don't get enough to eat? That is demagoguery, pure and simple, and you know it.

Mr. Lewis.   . . . and when you call me a demagogue, I will say you are less than a proper representative of the common people of this country when you do that.

The Chairman.   Now, Mr. Lewis, we don't stand for any sassy remarks to the members of this committee, and your rights will be protected here just the same as those of everybody else. I don't like that remark to a member of this committee.

Mr. Lewis.   Senator, did you object when the Senator called me a demagogue?

The Chairman.   Yes, it works both ways. I don't think the Senator should have called you a demagogue.[19]

The Truman Committee has been praised for the non-partisanship it displayed. While there was a lack of narrow partisanship in the usual sense, it is a mistake to laud the Committee as "non-partisan." Such thinking tends to reflect the American penchant for taking political matters out of politics. The Truman Committee was a political body, for no Congressional body can be non-political, nor should it be. However, it was a responsible political body.

But two of Truman's political friends found their way onto the committee staff, where they apparently did the jobs assigned to them. And occasionally partisan politics were injected into hearings, as were the considerations of the Senators for their constituents. Senator Carl A. Hatch and Lieutenant General Brehon B. Somervell exchanged words about the lack of Army camps in New Mexico, and Senator Mead put in a word for his state.[20] But these occurrences were few and relatively unimportant with respect to the whole work of the Committee. Furthermore, even these exceptions involved the real and important issue of geographical concentration of contracts. The measure of an American representative is not the extent to which he ignores the desires and needs of his own constituents, but his ability to meet these needs within a larger framework of the national interest.

REPORTS

The decision to make a report was made by the chairman and members. An outline was prepared by the chief counsel with the investigator's help. This was gone over by the Committee and then the report was drafted by the chief counsel, using material prepared by the investigator, usually a memorandum setting forth the salient facts. The Committee then "hammered it out again." [21]

Much has been made of the fact that the Truman Committee's reports were unanimous. Not until 1947 was a dissenting vote cast on a Committee report and not until 1948 was a minority report issued. The extraordinary unanimity of the reports enhanced their prestige and added to their impact on the agencies involved and on the public. There are several reasons why it was possible to get unanimity: the homogeneity of the membership, the solid factual foundation of the investigations, the practice of keeping members informed, the distribution of duties among all members. The mechanics involved the "hammering out" of outlines and drafts in sessions in "Harry's Doghouse"

and the practice of withholding a report until unanimity could
be achieved. Occasionally this resulted in delays until a recal-
citrant member could be brought around. One report on manpower was delayed for months because Senator Ferguson
refused to sign it.[22] These cases were exceptional, however, and
reports were usually presented to the Senate within a month or
so of the hearings. Undoubtedly reports were "watered down"
somewhat in the process of getting a draft that would be acceptable to all members, at least on controversial issues such as labor
and manpower where there was a marked divergence of views
among the members. Whether any such loss of vigor was com-
pensated by an increase in respect accorded the reports because
of their unanimity is impossible to determine. It is the judgment
of the writer that it was. But there is nothing to be gained from
unanimity for its own sake, and on the few occasions when
there were one or two recalcitrants it might have been better to
issue a report with a dissent than to "water it down" to meet the
objections of one member. It must be recognized, however, that
this might have made unanimity more difficult to achieve in
other cases.

One of the Committee's practices in issuing reports was an
important factor in its reputation for fairness. After the Committee had agreed on a draft of the report it was sent to the
Government Printing Office and a large number of galley proofs
were obtained. A copy of the report was then sent to each government agency, corporation, and individual affected by the report with a request for prompt comment. All facts that were
questioned (and the replies did come) were carefully rechecked
by Fulton and the staff, and all conclusions were reconsidered
before the report was finally adopted, although there were no
changes made in conclusions or recommendations unless factual
changes warranted them. "If there was still objection, the Committee would politely offer to hold an open hearing and accord

opportunity to prove the objection in public. Few ever availed themselves of this opportunity." [23]

This practice had the virtues of further ensuring the accuracy of the reports, giving the affected parties an opportunity to object and offer rebuttal, and giving the affected parties an opportunity to answer allegations publicly at the same time that the charges or allegations were made public in the report. In addition it permitted corrective action before the report was made public. The practice was extremely important in protecting the rights of individuals and in giving the Committee a high standing among even those government agencies which it had occasion to criticize.

After final adoption and printing, the report was presented to the Senate by the chairman or a designated member, usually a subcommittee chairman. Of the thirty-two reports presented during Truman's tenure as chairman, he presented fifteen and seventeen were presented by other members of the Committee. At the time of presentation each Senator was given a copy of the report; the press received copies a day or two in advance on a confidential basis to permit study. A copy was always sent or taken to the President a few days before presentation in order to inform him and to give him the opportunity to take remedial action.

RELATIONS WITH PRESS AND PUBLIC

The Committee's relations with the press were excellent and it received from the press exceptionally favorable treatment. Press relations were handled by Walter Hehmeyer, who issued periodic releases which were factual in content and restrained in tone. The Committee released its information as promptly as possible and in large measure avoided "leaks." No favoritism was shown, and release times were alternated to provide equal treatment for morning and afternoon papers. The press was briefed before the public hearings to help provide more intelligent coverage, and reports were given to the press in advance to permit study before public release.

The results were beneficial to the Committee, the press, and the public. The press and the public were given a "window" on the defense effort that would otherwise have been lacking. Not only did the Committee provide information through its own investigations of matters which otherwise would have remained untouched, but it put pressure on the defense agencies, particularly the military, to release information to the public. Although it accepted the word of the military as to what information would actually endanger the security of the country, the Committee forced justification of this judgment on numerous occasions, for it felt that much information was withheld not to protect security but to prevent criticism. The Committee itself was news, but it was also one of the most important sources of news about the war effort.

From the Committee's point of view, the generally favorable press it received enhanced its prestige and aided in carrying out its objective of bringing remedial action while the war was still in progress. An investigating committee not handling legislation is essentially an opinion-molding body, dependent for its success on its ability to create an effective public opinion with respect to the problems it tackles. The special investigating committee does not usually number among its members the really powerful men of Congress, who are more apt to devote their energies to the standing committees; also, it is subject to the vagaries of the legislative process if Congressional action is required to carry out its recommendations. It therefore must produce an effective public opinion to serve as a source of power and influence.

CONCLUSION

The Truman Committee meets very well the criteria for judging the effectiveness of an investigating committee set forth by Voorhis at the beginning of this chapter. Its chairman had the capabilities and character to serve effectively and well in that capacity. Its reports were prepared with care and the Committee was content to let the reports speak for it, without irresponsible interim statements by the chairman or members. Its staff was able and dedicated. Its deliberations were marked by a minimum of narrow partisanship and political bickering. And it adopted and observed fair and judicious rules of procedure.

It is worth noting that procedures constitute only one of the five criteria. Those who now tend to rely upon a uniform code of procedures as a means of curbing irresponsibility in Congressional committees misunderstand the relationship between responsibility and the procedures used. The Truman Committee's procedures were salutary because it was a responsible body, not vice versa. The adoption of a uniform code of procedure would be worthwhile, for it would be a formal recognition of the responsibility of Congress for the conduct of the committees which it creates and at least minimum standards would then be expected of all committees. But since all proposed codes have been based on the legal rights of the individual in the courtroom, the adoption of a uniform code of procedure is likely to result in some further formalizing of the courtroom pattern as a model for Congressional committees.

A code of procedures cannot be relied on alone to produce responsible and effective Congressional committees. Some elements of the Truman Committee's procedures, notably the submission of reports to affected parties before publication, were unique. But insofar as the Committee protected individuals, it did so by concentrating on conditions to be corrected rather than on individuals to be exposed or punished. Restraint and fairness are more important than adherence to prescribed legal procedures. For responsibility is compounded of intangibles in which substance is more important than form.

3) The Committee and Industrial Mobilization

We have fought to get you this job. We are going to fight to support you now in carrying it out. If you meet any obstacles in the carrying out of this job where this committee can turn the light of publicity on the subject or call attention to legislation that should be enacted to give you the necessary means to carry the job out, we want to be informed, and we are at your service.

Harry S Truman to Donald Nelson [1]

INTRODUCTION

When war broke out in Europe in 1939, United States planning for mobilizing the nation's industry was limited to the Industrial Mobilization Plan prepared by the Army in 1931 and revised by the Army and Navy Munitions Board in 1933, 1936, and 1939. Established primarily to coordinate Army and Navy procurement, the ANMB served to bring limited Navy participation in the process of planning which had been made the statutory responsibility of the Assistant Secretary of War. Although industrial mobilization planning would seem to be a civilian function, there was no civilian government agency with any interest in the subject and it was left to the services during the interwar period.

The 1939 revision of the Industrial Mobilization Plan proposed the establishment of a War Resources Administration as soon as war became imminent. The agency was to be responsible directly to the President, with authority to control the economy in his name. It was to be directed by a civilian administrator appointed by the President from among the "patriotic business leaders" of the country. He was to be assisted by an advisory council consisting of WRA staff members in charge of facilities, commodities, power, fuel, and transportation; representatives of the Secretaries of State, War, and Navy, and of the Army Chief of Staff and the Chief of Naval Operations; and representatives of supplementary emergency agencies which would be established to deal with selective service, finance, trade, labor, prices, and public relations. A series of industry committees was to effect liaison between the WRA and the various industries.[2]

The plan intended that the armed forces retain full responsibility for procurement with as little interference as possible. The War Resources Administration would coordinate military requirements with those of other government agencies and the civilian population. It would have responsibility for over-all production, distribution of available supplies, and administration of priorities and allocations of scarce goods and supplies.

The Industrial Mobilization Plan provided for separate agencies to deal with price control, selective service, labor, finance, trade, and public relations. But it was expected that these would only supplement the War Resources Administration, which would be the coordinating agency.

Although limited to the experience of World War I, the Industrial Mobilization Plan suffered a more serious political liability. It was prepared exclusively by military personnel. Just before the European war began an attempt was made to remedy this shortcoming by establishing a civilian board to consider the plan. On August 4, 1939, the establishment of a civilian advisory group named the War Resources Board was announced. Edward R. Stettinius, Jr., chairman of the board of the United States Steel Corporation, was named chairman of the War Resources Board, and he picked the following members: Karl T. Compton, president of the Massachusetts Institute of Technology; Walter S. Gifford, president of the American Telephone and Telegraph Company; John L. Pratt, a director of General Motors Corporation; Brigadier General Robert E. Wood, chairman of Sears, Roebuck & Company; and Dr. Harold G. Moulton, president of the Brookings Institution. John Hancock, a partner in the firm of Lehman Brothers and an associate of Bernard M. Baruch, was named to the Board in September. There was no representative of labor or agriculture.

The War Resources Board was promptly attacked for its big business bias, especially by spokesmen for labor and agriculture. The attack was helped by Stettinius' first statement, which began: "We of the business community . . ." [3] Roosevelt was quite cool to the Board and was apparently satisfied to have it file its reports and dissolve on November 24, 1939. The Board presented two reports, one to the President and one to the Army and Navy Munitions Board, neither of which was ever made public. In general, the Board approved the Industrial Mobilization Plan.

The President took no action with respect to the report. On September 8, 1939, he had proclaimed a state of limited national emergency and announced that the Executive Office should include an office for emergency management (although this was not activated). He had, in July, made the Munitions Board responsible directly to the President in order to retain control of mobilization planning. As the war in Europe passed through the winter with little action, no further steps were taken.

The Nazi offensive which swept across Europe in the spring of 1940 made it clear to many that the United States had to rearm quickly and on a large scale. Accordingly, the President activated the Office for Emergency Management on May 25, 1940. Its function was to coordinate the activities of the soon-to-be-established defense agencies with the policies of the President.

The next day the President announced the re-establishmnt of the Advisory Commission to the Council of National Defense, authorized during World War I. Since the Commission was purely advisory in function and no legislation was required, it presented the smallest possible target for isolationist and anti-war sentiment. It also had the advantage of being fully under the control of the President, who was still reluctant to turn over direction of the economy to another.

The Advisory Commission consisted of William S. Knudsen, president of General Motors Corporation, for industrial production; Sidney Hillman of the Amalgamated Clothing Workers of America, for employment; Stettinius for industrial materials; Leon Henderson, New Deal economist with extensive government experience, for prices; Chester C. Davis, with a farm community background and government agricultural experience, for farm products; Ralph Budd, president of the Chicago, Burlington & Quincy Railroad and president of the Association of American Railroads, for transportation; and Harriet Elliott, a leading professional woman, for consumer interests. A month later Donald M. Nelson, executive vice-president of Sears, Roebuck & Company, was appointed Coordinator of National Defense Purchases with a status virtually the same as that of a Commission member.

The Advisory Commission assembled a staff and became an operating agency. By the end of 1940 it had obtained "a number of powers, both *de jure* and *de facto,* that were strikingly similar to those contemplated for the War Resources Administration during a period when the Nation was not actually at war." [4]

The most important power exercised by the Advisory Commission was the power vested in Knudsen and Nelson to clear contracts. The President had earlier directed the Secretary of the Treasury to take over clearance of major defense contracts; this function was now delegated to the Advisory Commission, which cleared contracts in excess of $500,000. Knudsen and Nelson divided this function, Knudsen clearing contracts for "hard goods," Nelson clearing those for "soft goods." Congress added its approval on June 26 when it authorized the War and Navy Departments to expend certain funds and enter into contracts only "upon the recommendation of the Council of National Defense, and the Advisory Commission thereof, and with the approval of the President." [5] There was some ambiguity about the extent of this power, but it was exercised. The NDAC also certified defense facilities for accelerated tax amortization, certified defense cases to the Attorney General for antitrust exemption, and administered the power which had been given the President to assign priorities to national defense contracts.

With his appointment as Administrator of Priorities in October, 1940, Nelson emerged as the key man in the NDAC. The major shortcoming of the Advisory Commission was that it was a body of independent advisors to the President with no effective means of coordinating the efforts of its members. Nelson's responsibilities were such that he was able to some extent to serve a coordinating function. As the Commission divided into factions Nelson exerted a moderating influence, since each group preferred him to the others.[6]

During 1940 the NDAC performed many useful functions in spite of its shortcomings. Relying upon persuasion and personal influence, the Commission began a $9 billion expansion of the nation's industrial facilities, laid the foundation for later policies in many areas, and taught the armed services much about the technicalities of procurement. But the need for centralized direction demanded a new agency.

The President announced the establishment of the Office of Production Management on December 20, 1940. Still reluctant (or politically unable) to put the power in one man, he put the OPM under the direction of two men; Knudsen was named Director General and Hillman was named Associate Director General. These two, plus the Secretaries of War and Navy, constituted an OPM Council to serve as the policy-making body.

The OPM took over most of the functions and staff of the Advisory Commission and the rest were given to various other agencies. The Advisory Commission gradually ceased to function.

The Office of Production Management was organized functionally, with a Division of Production, a Division of Purchases (under Nelson), and a Defense Priorities Board. Until a reorganization in June, 1941, these Divisions operated rather independently of each other, as had been the case with the Advisory Commission.

The powers of the OPM were much more specific than those of the NDAC, however. It was given the power to formulate and execute all measures required for national defense production, to plan for industrial mobilization, and to create additional facilities where necessary. It had the power to coordinate the placement of major defense orders and contracts and to assign priorities. It did not have the power to determine requirements, military or otherwise, or to place contracts.

THE TRUMAN COMMITTEE AND OPM

The Truman Committee was established on March 1, 1941. It held its first hearings on April 15. Although the camp construction program and the distribution of defense contracts were the problems which had led Truman to introduce his resolution, the

Committee began its hearings with a general investigation of the state of the defense program. Secretary of War Henry L. Stimson, Under Secretary of War Robert P. Patterson, Secretary of the Navy Frank Knox, Knudsen, and Hillman were the first witnesses. All presented general statements about the defense program and their own particular responsibilities in it. Stimson testified that he was required by executive order to have contracts in excess of $500,000 cleared by OPM.[7] Knudsen, however, stated that he believed that OPM clearance was only advisory and not binding on the services.[8] The Committee showed great interest in service procedures in negotiating contracts (which had been authorized by Congress in 1940) and particularly in the cost-plus-a-fixed-fee contract, which seemed to be costing the government large sums of money. Some hint of future criticism was given by Senator Brewster, who vigorously questioned all four members of the OPM Council on the desirability of having a mobilization agency with a single head. All affirmed that the OPM was working well at the time.

As the Committee turned its attention to the camp construction program, the aluminum shortage, and the shipbuilding program, the Office of Production Management noted that "the investigation is proving to be more detailed and of longer duration than had been anticipated." [9] The burden of Congressional investigation led John Lord O'Brian, OPM's general counsel, to require clearance through his office of all OPM communications with Congress, a procedure which pleased none of the committees.

Although the Truman Committee investigated a number of specific programs of the defense effort, it returned again and again to the general subject of defense contracts, particularly their distribution. From these studies the Committee gradually assembled a picture of OPM's deficiencies.

These deficiencies stemmed primarily from a lack of power

and from a lack of centralization of authority within OPM, which frequently resulted in indecision. There were also differences of opinion within OPM and other agencies concerned with the defense effort about how far and how fast to go in conversion. Nelson, Stacy May (OPM chief statistician), and Leon Henderson (now head of the Office of Price Administration and Civilian Supply, which was outside OPM) were leaders of those who believed that civilian production would have to be cut back to a much greater degree than that contemplated by Knudsen.

Knudsen's knowledge and contacts in industry had been of great value during the period when the defense program was beginning and had to be accomplished by voluntary means. As the tempo of the program accelerated and began to impinge on civilian production, his business affiliations tended to become a liability, for he was reluctant to interfere with "business as usual." Defense spending was producing boom conditions which industry was loathe to abandon for the uncertainties of defense work except where that work supplemented normal production. Orders piled up in big companies, often waiting for government-financed facilities expansion, while the facilities of small ones went unused, bringing hundreds of letters of protest to Congressmen. Congressional attitudes on this subject were confirmed in July, 1941, when OPM released figures showing that almost 75 per cent of the Army and Navy supply contracts had gone to fifty-six companies and that six companies (Bethlehem Steel, General Motors, New York Shipbuilding Corporation, Curtiss-Wright, Newport News Shipbuilding & Drydock Company, and du Pont) held 31.3 per cent of the total.[10] This report did not indicate the extent of subcontracting, but it confirmed the conviction that contracts were not being spread.

More serious was reluctance on the part of important industries to undertake defense work. Both the steel and aluminum industries resisted OPM efforts to expand capacity, even at government expense. But it was the conduct of his own industry which made it impossible for Knudsen to continue in the top mobilization post after Pearl Harbor. The automobile industry was having its biggest year in 1941, and it resisted all attempts by OPM to cut back production, including the order to reduce production 20 per cent for the year beginning August 1, 1941. Although the industry accepted contracts for war materials, automobile production was not significantly reduced until after Pearl Harbor.

OPM relations with the armed services were rather difficult, primarily because of the lack of clear definition of functions. One area where the responsibility was clear enough was in the determination of military requirements. Throughout 1941 OPM tried to secure from the services "a clear-cut statement of program objectives, translatable into feasible production schedules for raw materials, components, and end products." [11] OPM did not receive such a statement until after Pearl Harbor.

This failure of the services resulted from a number of factors. They did not know what kind of war they might have to fight. Earlier planning had been based on the assumption that the military mission would be to defend American territory. By 1941 this assumption appeared inadequate, but, on the other hand, Congressional and public opinion did not seem to support planning that went further; that summer the House of Representatives voted to extend the draft by a margin of only one vote, and that only as the result of a tremendous effort by Speaker Sam Rayburn. Another factor was the constantly accelerating pace of the program, including the expansion of foreign aid under lend-lease. But the services labored under the delusion that "all shortages could be made up simply by dipping a little deeper into the civilian economy." [12] OPM officials tried to disabuse military officials of this delusion, largely without success. OPM officials also tried throughout 1941 to get the Army and Navy to increase their estimates of requirements for many items of equipment; although this was not strictly a function of OPM, Knudsen, Nelson, and others were convinced that service requirements were going to be much greater than was being anticipated. In this judgment they were entirely correct.

Other difficulties centered on procurement and priorities. The Office of Production Management had authority to clear major contracts, but Nelson lacked the power to decide disputes between his office and the services, although he tried to get this power in January, 1941. Nor did the contract clearance procedure work very well. The Army and Navy refused to use a standard clearance request form and frequently provided inadequate information for OPM action. OPM commodity specialists frequently gave contracts only a cursory review, at least in part because the contracts were presented ready for signing, leaving the agency little opportunity to make a constructive contribution. Nor did OPM have any effective means of checking the actual contract against the clearance requests. As James W. Fesler observed, "The Armed Services, in short, remained for all practical purposes autonomous with respect to procurement." [13]

By the summer of 1941 priorities had become a serious problem. Power to assign priorities had been given to OPM, but staff difficulties and a lack of understanding led OPM to give up civilian control over military priorities by turning their assignment over to the Army and Navy Munitions Board. The system itself was unworkable, however, for there was no control over the quantities of goods for which priorities could be assigned. The result was that holders of priorities competed for materials that in many cases were not available in sufficient quantities to supply them all. Furthermore, powerful civilian producers, such as the automobile industry, succeeded in accumulating supplies despite lack of priorities. The problem was further complicated by increasing foreign aid requirements and the necessity of some kind of priority for essential civilian production.

In an effort to solve the problem of priorities, Roosevelt on August 28, 1941, established the Supply Priorities and Allocations Board as a policy-making and coordinating agency for the defense program. Headed by Vice-President Henry A. Wallace, it included as members the Secretaries of War and Navy; the Director General and Associate Director General of OPM; the President's assistant on defense aid abroad, Harry L. Hopkins; and Leon Henderson, head of the new Office of Price Administration (the civilian supply part of his former agency was returned to the Office of Production Management). Nelson was appointed Executive Director of SPAB, and OPM became an operating arm of the new Board. SPAB provided a central point for priorities decisions and its work led up to the allocations approach to the distribution of materials, but it was an administrative monstrosity with confused lines of responsibility. Nelson, for example, gave orders to Hillman and Knudsen as Executive Director of SPAB; as head of a division in OPM he was their subordinate.

It was apparent to most observers that the defense organization was inadequate, but nothing was done until after Pearl Harbor. The Truman Committee's hammering at the problem of small business did bring some results. The Committee's concern with the question reflected Congressional attention to the problems of constituents; Congressional mail was flooded with complaints from small businessmen back home. Truman told one witness, "If you should see my correspondence, you would think that every little businessman in the country is going out of business." [14] The pressure brought some changes in OPM and more attention to the problem by OPM and the services, but small business was never fully integrated into the war effort and remained a problem throughout the war. OPM gave the Committee some credit for the early steps taken; the Committee was told that assistance was given "by the thought that your committee has given to this problem and by some of the facts brought out regarding the importance of maximum distribution. . . . The efforts of this committee have been very constructive . . ." [15] It may be added that the Committee had little success with either OPM or the services when it took up specific contracts in which there appeared to be discrimination against or disregard of small business.[16]

After Pearl Harbor it became obvious that drastic changes would have to be made in the organization for industrial mobilization. The Truman Committee's careful assembling of its picture of OPM deficiencies contributed greatly to this understanding. The President's announcement of the changes coincided with the presentation of the Truman Committee's First Annual Report on January 15, 1942. The report was a major factor in at least the timing of the reorganization.

The report was a devastating indictment of OPM. Truman presented it to the Senate:

> Standing up straight behind his desk in the back row, he adjusted his spectacles and occasionally tugged at a button on the coat of his grey suit. As he read a summarized account of the committee's findings his voice was almost inaudible. He spoke rapidly. It was not a dramatic presentation, but Senators on both sides of the nearly empty chamber began to move over to where Truman was standing. Small groups crowded around to hear his words.[17]

The drama was in the report. It was lengthy and covered virtually all subjects the Committee had looked into in the preceding nine months. But the most important sections dealt with the OPM and the over-all job of mobilizing the economy for war. Its discussion of OPM began:

The task of correlating and administering most of the defense and war production program has been entrusted to the Office of Production Management, which was especially created for that purpose. Its record has not been impressive; its mistakes of commission have been legion; and its mistakes of omission have been even greater. It has all too often done nothing when it should have realized that problems cannot be avoided by refusing to admit that they exist. In an emergency of this kind where Government leadership and planning is an absolute essential, the OPM should have adopted the old Army maxim that "in an emergency it is better to do any intelligent act than to do nothing at all."

. . . the disappointing record of the Office of Production Management is not so much due to its lack of power as to its failure to perform the functions for which it was created . . .

In those instances where it has failed, the failure has not been due so much to the lack of power as to the ineptness of the officials of the Office of Production Management and their unwillingness to use the weapon which they had . . .

. . . the usual procedure was to refrain from raising the issue and to avoid responsibility by claiming lack of authority and, if possible, by referring the matter to some other agency of Government.[18]

The report added some vigorous criticisms of an OPM institution to which the Committee attributed many of its difficulties:

The principal positions of the Office of Production Management were assigned to persons holding important positions with large companies who were willing and anxious to serve on a dollar per year, or without compensation (w.o.c.) basis. They usually did not sever their business connections, but instead obtained leave of absence. In many instances they continued to act for their companies, publicly announcing that their Government work was part-time only. Their companies continued to pay their salaries. In some cases their compensation was even increased. . . .

Although the contracts obtained by the companies loaning the services of dollar-a-year and w.o.c men are not passed upon by the men so loaned, such companies do obtain very substantial benefits from the practice. . . .

All important procurement contracts must be approved by these dollar-a-year and w.o.c. men, which means that contracts must conform to their theories of business. Since they represent the largest companies, this means that the defense program in all its ramifications must obtain the approval of the large companies. This does not mean that the boards of directors of the large companies are requested to determine the defense program, nor does it even mean that the dollar-a-year and w.o.c. men consciously favor their companies or their companies' methods of doing business. On the contrary, the committee believes that most dollar-a-year and w.o.c. men are honest and conscientious, and that they would not intentionally favor big business. However, it is not their intentional acts that the committee fears, but their subconscious tendency, without which they would hardly be human, to judge all matters before them in the light of their past experience and convictions.

It is only natural that such men should believe that only companies of the size and type with which they were associated have the ability to perform defense contracts; that small and intermediate companies ought not to be given prime contracts; that the urgencies of the defense program are such that they have no time to consider small companies for defense contracts; that the large companies ought not to be required to subcontract items which they could profitably manufacture and as to which they express lack of confidence in the productive facilities of smaller concerns; that the producers of strategic materials should not be expected or required to increase their capacities, even at Government expense, where that might result in excess capacity after the war and adversely affect their postwar profits; and that large companies should not be expected or required to convert their existing facilities into defense plants, where they prefer to use their plants to make the profits from their civilian business and, at the same time, to have additional plants directly or indirectly paid for by the Government, which they can operate profitably on terms dictated by themselves. . . .

The committee is opposed to a policy of taking free services from persons with axes to grind, and the committee believes that the Government should not continue to accept the loan of dollar-a-year and w.o.c. men by companies with so large a stake in the defense program. . . . No man can honestly serve two masters.[19]

The report noted the need of a single man to direct the program and suggested that it might be necessary to create a new department or agency to be responsible for the entire production program. It also noted that Senator Kilgore had introduced a bill, for which there was a certain amount of public support, to create a Department of Supply.

Several days before his presentation to the Senate, Truman took a copy of the report to the White House. Apparently this was the final prod that goaded Roosevelt into action because on the evening of January 13, 1942, before the report was made public, he announced the establishment of the War Production Board, headed by Nelson, whose "decision as to questions of procurement and production will be final." [20]

Roosevelt had been considering an organization like the WPB for several months. His first choice for the man to head it was Supreme Court Justice William O. Douglas, and apparently he talked to Douglas about it. But Hopkins talked him into appointing Nelson, whom the President did not know very well.[21] James F. Byrnes warned the President, "The man will last only as long as it is recognized that he has your complete confidence." [22]

Nelson was given the opportunity to draft the executive order setting up the WPB. He outlined the powers that he wanted to John Lord O'Brian, general counsel of OPM and WPB, and O'Brian drafted the order.[23] It was signed by the President and promulgated on January 16, 1942. It contained a sweeping grant of power. The Board itself, with the same membership as the SPAB, was advisory only. The administrative and policy-making powers were vested in the chairman (Nelson), who, with the advice and assistance of the members, was directed to:

(1) Exercise general direction over the war procurement and production program.

(2) Determine the policies, plans, procedures, and methods of the several Federal departments, establishments, and agencies in respect to war procurement and production, including purchasing, contracting, specifications, and construction; and including conver-

sion, requisitioning, plant expansion, and the financing thereof; and issue such directives in respect thereto as he may deem necessary or appropriate.

The authority of the WPB over the other agencies was stated:

(3) Federal departments, establishments, and agencies shall comply with the policies, plans, methods, and procedures in respect to war procurement and production as determined by the Chairman; and shall furnish to the Chairman such information relating to war procurement and production as he may deem necessary for the performance of his duties.

(4) The Army and Navy Munitions Board shall report to the President through the Chairman of the War Production Board.

(5) The Chairman may exercise the powers, authority, and discretion conferred upon him by this Order through such officials or agencies and in such manner as he may determine; and his decisions shall be final.[24]

A week later the President abolished the OPM and transferred all its functions and powers to the WPB. On April 7, the President delegated to the Chairman of the WPB the allocation authority granted the President in the Second War Powers Act. Each of these executive orders affirmed the authority of the chairman over the production and procurement program.

THE TRUMAN COMMITTEE AND THE WPB

Actually Nelson did not have the power implied in the executive orders. His decisions were not self-executing but had to be enforced on other agencies, and their cooperation was very important. Nelson was not an intimate of Roosevelt and lacked assurance that the President would back him up. This fact was recognized by other officials and encouraged them to take differences to the President not as an appeal from a decision by constituted authority but as equals seeking a decision from an arbiter. Also, the Secretaries of War and Navy, as Cabinet members, saw the President regularly, while Nelson did not.

Nelson had the confidence of the President in a general way but lacked the kind of confidence that Byrnes had told the President he must have—the kind of confidence that later was Byrnes's source of strength as head of OWM. Byrnes was able to make his decisions the equivalent of Presidential decisions, and everyone knew it.

Nelson's source of political strength was not the President but Hopkins. He dissipated this strength, however, by neglecting his contacts with Hopkins, a mistake that Lieutenant General Brehon B. Somervell (who was also a friend of Hopkins) did not make.

Nelson's character and personality have been the subject of speculation by virtually every writer on the politics of wartime Washington.[25] He brought great assets to his almost impossible task. He had a keen grasp of the complexities of the American economy and of the central problems of war production, which is what made Roosevelt willing to give him the job. He understood the interrelationship "between a fully productive economy and the objective of maximum output of military goods." [26] He had a feel for the kind and extent of controls which the people of the country wanted and would accept (in marked contrast to Patterson and Somervell), which influenced members of the Truman Committee to believe him the ablest of the OPM officials to appear before them.

He had very great patience, and would carefully hear and weigh all opinions before acting; even then he preferred persuasion to coercion. He organized the WPB to include a wide variety of opinion. But he preferred dissenting elements (in and out of WPB) to settle differences themselves without his having to step in. This meant "a tendency to let matters drift to a crisis," [27] although he then could take vigorous action.

He was insensitive to details of administration, however. He was not interested in problems not directly concerned with broad policy. This was a shortcoming that led to much friction with General Somervell, head of the Army Service Forces, who was deeply concerned with administrative detail and who could not understand this lack in Nelson. "Nelson was not aggressive about his jurisdiction and his powers," Fesler comments. "He allowed ANMB to elude his grasp, although it was subordinate to him, and he permitted the War Department's Services of Supply, over which he said he had control, to become something decidedly other than what he thought it ought to be." [28]

In short, Nelson was admirably equipped for policy-making, both in talent and temperament, and poorly equipped for supervising its execution. Unfortunately, his job required both. In fairness it must be noted, however, that the production achievement accomplished under Nelson's leadership was tremendous.

To a considerable extent the Truman Committee substituted Congressional confidence in Nelson for that necessary degree of Presidential confidence, and it substantially bolstered his power. Relations with OPM had not been happy (apparently there was even an attempt by some OPM officials in January of 1942 to put the Truman Committee out of business by getting the Senate to cut off funds). Relations with WPB were excellent. Nelson honestly believed he should conduct his office "in a goldfish bowl," and he received a sympathetic hearing from the Truman Committee. The WPB cooperated fully with the Committee, turning over documents and other information about its activities. Nelson's liaison officer, Edwin A. Locke, Jr., kept the Committee continuously informed of events in WPB. Frequently the Committee was able to obtain material from the WPB which had been denied it by the War Department on grounds of security. There was a mutual respect between the Committee and Nelson, even when they differed on policy, which was a source of strength to the WPB and which made a real contribution to the war effort.

The harmony between them was apparent from Nelson's first appearance before the Committee on January 28, 1942. Nelson, appearing at his request to explain his policies with respect to dollar-a-year men, stated that he would like to staff WPB with business executives on that basis because of obligations which prevented their working for much lower government salaries. He told the Committee that he was tightening up the restrictions on their use and laid down the following rules by which WPB would abide:

1. No person shall be appointed on a dollar-a-year basis unless he is a man of outstanding business or technical ability, of unimpeachable integrity, and especially qualified for the work for which he is chosen.

2. No dollar-a-year man shall be appointed to any position if, with reasonable effort, a man equally qualified can be found and induced to come here to fill such position on a regular Government salary.

3. No person shall be employed in any position in which he will make decisions affecting the affairs of his own company.

4. No appointment shall be made except after a thorough investigation of the proposed appointee by one of the investigating agencies of the government.[29]

The Committee differed strongly with Nelson, feeling that businessmen should be as willing as others to make sacrifices, but Truman spoke for the Committee when he told Nelson:

I am not going to argue this question with you, because I have certain views on it and you have certain views. We are behind you to win this war, and I say, whether you are right or wrong, we are going to get behind you and help you win it.[30]

Truman also promised the Committee's help and indicated the Committee's proprietary interest in WPB:

We have fought to get you this job. We are going to fight to support you now in carrying it out. If you meet any obstacles in the carrying out of this job where this committee can turn the light of publicity on the subject or call attention to legislation that should be enacted to give you the necessary means to carry the job out, we want to be informed, and we are at your service.[31]

The dollar-a-year man issue came up again in connection with the question of whether the War Production Board was proceeding rapidly enough in the conversion of industry. "Business-as-usual" attitudes did not automatically disappear after Pearl Harbor, and WPB conversion measures proceeded against a certain amount of industry resistance—the consumer's durable goods industries were not fully shut down until the end of May, 1942. On March 14 the resignation of Robert R. Guthrie raised the issue as to whether these attitudes extended into WPB. Guthrie was head of the WPB textile, leather, and clothing branch, and he resigned with a public denunciation of Philip D. Reed (chairman of the board of the General Electric Company and chief of the WPB Bureau of Industry Branches) and other WPB personnel for delaying conversion by being "industry minded." Nelson asked the Truman Committee to investigate the charges, which it did.[32] A report was issued on June 18.[33] The Committee was not impressed "with Mr. Reed's ability or accomplishments" but recognized that there were in WPB two approaches to the problem of conversion: one advocating immediate and drastic curtailment of civilian production for which war work would be substituted; the other advocating a more gradual replacement of civilian production as war orders were placed with the firms. It did not support Guthrie's charges as to motivation, but held that conversion had not proceeded rapidly enough and that the attitudes of dollar-a-year men were in part responsible. It recommended that the rule that such men could not make decisions affecting their own companies be extended to cover their own industries. The report suggested that the Guthrie charges might have performed a useful service by raising an issue that had resulted in speeding up conversion to the point where it was then proceeding satisfactorily. It recognized that the issue of dollar-a-year men was partly a matter of personal integrity which could not be governed by a formula, and the issue was not raised again by the Committee.

This report occasioned the sharpest criticism of the Committee which Nelson made, although he did not make it publicly. Two days before the report was issued, Nelson, having received the customary advance copy, wrote Truman a letter which was bitterly critical of the entire report on the Guthrie charges and concluded: "I again express regret that your Committee should undertake, at this time, to put out a report so inaccurate in its statements of fact and so ill-considered in its conclusions." [34]

Nelson seems to have recognized, however, that the differences between the Committee and himself stemmed from differences in their attitudes toward the use of dollar-a-year men, and he did not make a public issue of the matter.

A more important question facing Nelson when he took over the chairmanship of WPB was what to do about military procurement. He had the authority to take over military procurement, and he was aware that a majority of the members of Congressional committees with whom he had had contact wanted procurement placed in one agency under civilian control.[35] Had he decided to do so, he would have had the full support of the Truman Committee.[36]

He decided that the military should retain procurement in their own hands. He gives several reasons for this decision: (1) Baruch's warning not to let dollar-a-year men place contracts because of their vulnerability to criticism; (2) the time that it would take to set up a new procurement agency and the resulting delay in war production; (3) the difficulty in separating procurement from inspection of finished products as to conformity with design and specifications, which Nelson felt had to remain with the military; (4) the time-consuming task of unraveling the legal tangle that would be involved in making the transfer.[37] He did not add that the inevitable political battle with the services was something he did not want to provoke.

It is difficult to quarrel with this decision. Whatever case there was for a Ministry of Supply was greatly weakened by the situation in January, 1942. What is less understandable is the casual way in which Nelson not only failed to strengthen his power of contract clearance but virtually gave it away. Nelson in practice delegated clearance authority to the procurement agencies and, although he placed deputies in the agencies, his control was lost. The Contract Review Branch of WPB audited the contracts after placement but did not clear them during the negotiation stage.[38]

The centralizing of control in WPB was paralleled by similar developments within the armed forces. On January 30, 1942, the Navy established an Office of Procurement and Material to act as a coordinating agency for Naval procurement matters. It was headed by Rear Admiral Samuel M. Robinson, and was under the cognizance of Under Secretary James V. Forrestal.[39] On March 9, in a general reorganization of the War Department, the material and service branches of the Army were combined in a Services of Supply (later the Army Service Forces) under the command of General Somervell.[40] While these changes were dictated in part by the responsibiities of the services, it is probable that the purpose had a political element—to strengthen their position vis-à-vis the War Production Board.[41]

On March 12, an agreement was signed by Nelson and Under Secretary of War Patterson setting forth the relationships and responsibilities of the WPB, the Services of Supply, and the Army Air Forces Material Command. A similar agreement was signed with the Navy on April 22. In essence these agreements left with the services the responsibility for "purchase, including the negotiation, placement, and administration of contracts," and recognized the responsibility of WPB for over-all policy, planning, allocation, and scheduling.[42]

Explaining these developments to the Truman Committee in April, Nelson termed the agreement "the Magna Carta of our operation." This attitude was shared by Somervell and Patterson, although for different reasons. Nelson believed that the agreement embodied the "fundamental concept" that the "war supply organizations should be viewed by all participants as a single integrated system operating under the general direction of the Chairman of the War Production Board." [43] The Committee was not entirely satisfied, and in June questioned Nelson rather sharply as to whether he was retaining control. Truman told Nelson that "we want to have this thing in the hands of civilians, not in the hands of the 'brass hats.' " A few minutes later he repeated, "What I want to do is be sure that the responsibility stays in your hands, for I have confidence in you, and I think you can successfully do the job. Don't let it get away from you." [44]

Nelson's hopes were not realized. There were conflicts with the services, especially with Somervell, throughout the war. In part these resulted from personality conflicts; in part from the fact that relationships were determined by specific issues (such as priorities, allocations, production) rather than by formal agreement; in part by the institutional responsibilities of the WPB and the services, which inevitably impinged on each other; and in part by Nelson's dilution of his authority. Some of these conflicts were avoidable; some were not.

Nelson tended to view these conflicts as resulting from Army attempts to control the civilian economy, an explanation that is too simple. Somervell was a brilliant administrator, with a passion for administrative detail. He was hard-driving, aggressive, even ruthless in meeting opposition. Single-minded in doing a job, he was impatient with any consideration that impinged on his work.[45] He especially hated indecisiveness. He tended to view the operation of the civilian agencies with which he came in conflict as part of an attempt by "Henry Wallace and the leftists to take over the country." [46] In this category he included the Truman Committee, which he characterized as "formed in iniquity for political purposes," alleging that the Committee was established to punish him for refusing to do a favor for Truman when Somervell was in charge of construction.[47]

Somervell doubtless had no conscious desire to take over the economy, but his efforts to subordinate all other considerations to his mission of supplying the Army left him vulnerable to such charges. In May of 1942 he sent Nelson a proposal for the reorganization of his command and the WPB "which would have (1) placed the apportionment of materials for the essential civilian economy under the military, and (2) assigned to the military responsibility for the establishment of policies to govern resources mobilization, use, and apportionment." [48] Somervell was engaged in building an organization which substantially duplicated that of WPB, and he wanted to mesh them together. Nelson rejected the proposal with a sharp letter, saying, "The battle of production is the primary responsibility of the chairman of the WPB in much the same sense that military battles are the primary responsibility of the military chiefs." [49]

Not all of Nelson's difficulties were with the armed forces. His dilution of the powers of WPB led to the creation of a number of new agencies with overlapping functions and authority, largely outside the control of WPB. A number of "czars" were set up to handle specific programs—petroleum, solid fuels, rubber. Nelson's worst error in this respect was his approval of the creation of the War Manpower Commission outside WPB. The President asked him if he wished a separate agency or if he wished to retain control of manpower within the WPB; Nelson chose the independent agency.[50] Public controversies occurred between the WPB and these agencies as well as the Army, and they quarreled among themselves. Each time that Nelson had to take a dispute to the President, or was unable to resolve one, it became clearer that WPB was not performing the function of over-all direction of the domestic war effort but was being placed in the position of equality in contention. In November, at a press conference, the President answered a question as to whether the military or the WPB had the final say on production schedules and materials allocations by saying, "They are supposed to agree. And if they don't agree, then I'll put them in a room and I'll say, 'No food until you come out in agreement.' " [51]

They neither agreed nor starved. In September a reorganization of WPB was effected; Ferdinand Eberstadt became Program Vice-Chairman with authority to institute the Controlled Materials Plan, which became the basis of raw materials allocation for the balance of the war. Eberstadt brought the needed administrative skill, drive, and decisiveness to WPB, but he was regarded as inclined toward the services. Presumably his appointment was to appease the services as well as to regain WPB control of priorities and allocations. A few days before, Nelson announced the formation of a Production Executive Committee under the chairmanship of Charles E. Wilson, president of General Electric Company. In part, this was probably an attempt to offset the influence of Eberstadt. Wilson and Eberstadt were the only civilian members of PEC; the others were the top procurement officers of the Army, Navy, Air Forces, Maritime Commission, and the Naval Air Forces. Nelson's objective was to regain control of production, particularly scheduling, which was to be a major function of PEC.

A prolonged controversy over the scheduling power took place in the fall of 1942. Wilson was determined to carry out the mission given him by Nelson. Somervell and Patterson carried to the President their case against giving Wilson this power. Roosevelt called in Nelson, who explained the fight and turned down an offer of Presidential assistance with the admonition, "Don't help the other fellow." [52] The President finally directed Stimson, Knox, and Nelson to settle the issue. Since Nelson's view of the necessity for scheduling as a means of fitting production into the limits of available resources and of his responsibility for this coincided with Stimson's view of the functions of WPB, an agreement was reached in December which gave authority to the Chairman of PEC to direct the scheduling of the various production programs.

During this controversy Somervell went to Admiral William D. Leahy, the President's personal Chief of Staff, and tried to persuade him that Nelson should be fired at once. Leahy rejected the proposal and later commented:

. . . The War Production Board was doing a good job considering the difficulties it faced. I had the impression that Somervell was trying to expand his own operations radically—with the best of intentions. Two groups were mixing into war production—the Army and WPB—and that was the trouble. It was the duty of the Joint Chiefs to make war plans and there was an appropriate agency charged with procuring the things necessary to implement the war plans. I could see no merit in Somervell's recommendation. The high command had been furnished all the necessary supplies and equipment for our first major offensive—the invasion of North Africa— which was then proceeding satisfactorily.[53]

Early in 1943 a difficult conflict developed between Wilson and Eberstadt concerning jurisdiction over the industry and staff division of WPB. There was logic in both positions and the issue was probably insoluble. Nelson let the matter drift for too long. In February, Stimson, Knox, and Byrnes, now Economic Stabilizer, convinced Roosevelt that he should fire Nelson and appoint Baruch as his successor. A letter was sent to Baruch inviting him to become the chairman of WPB.[54] Nelson was informed of this and moved quickly. On February 16, he demanded and received the resignation of Eberstadt, and then announced Wilson's appointment as Executive Vice-Chairman with broad authority over WPB operations. Roosevelt was pleased with this display of decisiveness and changed his mind.

Congress was well informed as to the developments of 1942, and there was severe criticism of the dispersal of WPB powers. Throughout 1942, the Tolan Committee was publicly taking WPB to task for transferring its powers over procurement and production to the armed services and urging either that the WPB exercise its powers or that its functions be given to a new civilian agency. In October this Committee told the House, "The present dispersal of responsibility for production has been actively promoted by the War Production Board," and recommended that Congress establish an Office of War Mobilization.[55]

The Truman Committee was gentler with Nelson personally but equally critical of the results. In private the Committee repeatedly urged Nelson to retain control of the powers he had been given and to "get tough." On September 14, Truman made a report to the Senate in which he stated:

Mr. Nelson has tried hard to do his job, and the committee expresses only admiration for his intentions and his abilities. The committee does not want anyone to make the mistake of thinking that it is critical of Mr. Nelson. It is not. But Mr. Nelson encountered, and is still encountering, because of obstruction not only in the various government departments but also in the Armed Forces, many difficulties in assuming and exercising the powers which the President and the members of the committee, and I think the entire Congress, desired Mr. Nelson to exercise.[56]

Both Senator Truman and Representative Tolan rather regretted that the Congress had not had an opportunity to discuss Senator Kilgore's bill to establish a Department of Supply (which had been dropped when the WPB was created). When

Tolan, Kilgore, and Claude D. Pepper introduced a bill to establish an Office of War Mobilization, Truman and Senator Murray joined them in seeking its enactment. There seemed to be no other way to achieve the centralized control which they deemed essential.

In its Second Annual Report, presented on March 11, 1943, the Truman Committee recapitulated the problem and found a note of hope in Nelson's recent efforts to regain his authority:

> Mr. Nelson appeared before the committee shortly after his appointment. The committee publicly urged Mr. Nelson to exercise vigorously the authority which the President had vested in him. Mr. Nelson informed the committee that he had sufficient authority to take any action that might be necessary, and that he proposed to exercise his powers and get the job done.
>
> Had Mr. Nelson proceeded accordingly, many of the difficulties with which he has been confronted in recent months might never have arisen. Instead, Mr. Nelson delegated most of his powers to the War and Navy Departments and to a succession of so-called czars. This made it difficult for him to exercise the functions for which he was appointed. At the same time, none of the separate agencies had sufficient authority to act alone.
>
> Recently, Mr. Nelson took steps to remedy this situation. The committee believes that the success of the program requires a strong central authority. Mr. Nelson was appointed for that purpose and should exercise all of the powers delegated to him.[57]

Congressional criticism of WPB was mounting. It came from several sources besides the Truman and Tolan Committees. On May 10, the Senate overwhelmingly passed a bill to set up an independent civilian supply agency, in spite of Nelson's resolute opposition. On May 6, in a report on conflicting war programs, the Truman Committee stated, "Today discussion of the overall legal authority of the War Production Board is mere pedantry. Although the authority may exist it has not been exercised." [58] A week later a subcommittee of the Senate Military Affairs

Committee recommended immediate action to create a War Mobilization Board, pending further hearings on the bill to establish an Office of War Mobilization.

Growing Congressional support for the War Mobilization bills and fear that the legislation would be too inflexible led Roosevelt to establish on May 27, 1943, an Office of War Mobilization under Byrnes.[59] Byrnes was given sweeping powers to enable him to exercise top-level coordination of the various war programs. In Fesler's words, "Except for the authority over manpower, all these were functions that had been originally entrusted to WPB but had atrophied from disuse or had shrunk under the pressure of resistance by other agencies to their exercise." [60]

The order was popular. Truman stated that his Committee had long advocated such "an agency with centralized authority." The choice of Byrnes was likewise popular. He established his office in the White House as a symbol of his authority and was able to exercise power effectively—over the armed services as well as the civilian agencies—when he chose to do so. Freed of its coordinating responsibilities, WPB continued as a vital operating agency for production, scheduling, and allocation of resources.

CONCLUSION

The authors of the most thorough and penetrating study of wartime production controls conclude:

By far the most important lesson is that the power to contract is the power to control. Optimum use of national resources for war purposes requires a planned integration of materials, facilities, labor, and management. Even if we assume that the nation is willing and prepared to make every sacrifice for war at the price of bankruptcy for the national economy, there is no assurance that undirected military procurement will provide the most effective and the largest war output. The secret of maximum war production lies in balanced output. There must be a balance between men and weapons, between munitions production and non-munitions production. All these factors must be brought into the most effective relationship and maintained in that status.

Unlimited and undirected procurement by the military services has proved to result not only in an unbalanced assignment of the factors of production, but also in wasteful duplication of effort.[61]

It is clear that the power to review contracts was initially given to civilian agencies, both by Presidential direction and by legislation. Nelson was aware of the importance of balanced production but seems not to have been fully aware of the importance of the review power, which was his only means of insuring balanced output. Consequently, the basic objective of balanced output was itself a matter of contention throughout the war.

Review by WPB was accomplished after the fact, when it was faced with an existing situation rather than a plan. This lack of control limited the success of even the Controlled Materials Plan, for while the procuring agencies were allotted the raw materials within the limits of their availability, the orders for end products requiring materials in excess of those allotted remained in the market, competing for components and other materials not directly controlled. "Since the actions associated with military procurement preceded the imposition of material and other controls during the war, the civilian agencies were constantly in the position of a fire department trying to put out a series of conflagrations with an inadequate supply of water." [62]

Congress in general, and the Truman and Tolan Committees in particular, seem to have grasped this fact more clearly than officials of the administrative branch of the government. Their insistence on civilian control was based more on the traditional distrust of the man in uniform than on a careful analysis of previous experience. This resulted in the proposal for a Department of Supply as the Congressional answer to the problem, with a consequent posing of the issue in terms of civilian contracting *or* military contracting and a diversion of attention from the alternative of military contracting coupled with effective civilian review of major contracts. A civilian contracting agency was not feasible, at least in 1942; but the power to review contracts was given away, apparently with scarcely a thought to its importance. In June, 1942, the Truman Committee questioned Nelson sharply as to whether he was really keeping the contract review power in his hands, but accepted his assurance that his arrangements with the services were workable.

However, a Congressional committee is limited in what it can do. It is impossible to force a man to wield power if he does not choose to do so. The Truman Committee repeatedly prodded Nelson to exercise the powers vested in him, sometimes in public, more frequently in private. It could do no more, beyond using its power to support him when he decided to follow the Committee's urging. The Committee's relations with the WPB and Nelson were conducted at a very high level. The Committee gave important support to a vital agency without either giving up its critical judgment or attempting to substitute its judgment for that of responsible administrators. And it should be noted that Committee criticisms were directed at agency actions and policies, not at individuals.

It is difficult to assess with any precision the Truman Committee's contribution to the accomplishments of the WPB. For the WPB was not a failure. It probably accomplished its operating job of production as well as could have been expected under the circumstances, as Admiral Leahy suggested. But it did have to fight for even such a basic concept as balanced production. And in its battles, the steadfast support of the Committee contributed an important element. The Committee helped create and maintain the public confidence WPB needed, since its operation depended so heavily upon voluntary compliance. To a significant degree, it did substitute its confidence in Nelson for the missing Presidential confidence, although we must acknowledge that Presidential confidence would have been more effective. But in 1942 the overriding need was for production, and the Truman Committee's support of Nelson and the WPB was a vital factor in the success of the WPB in meeting this need.

The WPB, however, was not successful in its role of coordinator of the war agencies. It never succeeded in giving over-all direction to the war effort. And when the failure was clear, it was Congress (prompted by the Truman Committee—its major source of information and analysis of the problem) which prodded the President into setting up an effective office for coordination. The Congressional remedy would have lumped most of the war agencies into a super-agency (a persistence of the Department of Supply idea) which probably would have been inflexible and unwieldy, but the Congressional instinct with respect to the need was sure.

4) The Committee and Conflicting War Production Programs

*I wish the job could be accomplished without these head-on colli-
sions. I believe that there are ways of maneuvering so that head-on
collisions can be avoided. It is my experience with businessmen in
government that they always get into these battles, not alone with
one another but with the heads of other government agencies. They
don't know how to administer the things they must administer as
well as the politicians know how.*

President Franklin D. Roosevelt [1]

THE DISPUTE

In August, 1942, President Roosevelt appointed a Rubber Survey Committee headed by Bernard M. Baruch. This was done
in part to mollify Congress for his veto of the bill establishing
an independent agency for the production of rubber. In part, it
was done to share the responsibility for the decision to ration
gasoline in order to conserve rubber. The oil industry and Petroleum Coordinator Harold Ickes were opposing gasoline rationing, and it was generally unpopular, but the War Production
Board regarded it as absolutely necessary as a rubber conservation measure. Baruch's committee relieved the President of
having to make the decision alone.

As a result of the Rubber Survey Committee's recommendations, the Office of Rubber Director was established in the WPB with broad powers over the rubber production program. William M. Jeffers, president of the Union Pacific Railroad, was named director. Jeffers was supposed to be under the control of Nelson; in fact he reported to the President with only nominal WPB direction. Jeffers was a tough, aggressive individual who gave little thought to other parts of the defense program. He was inclined to fight his battles in the press. He did an effective job of organizing synthetic rubber production after the program had been long delayed, but he did so at the cost of considerable friction with other agencies and some interference with other vital programs.

Another of the commodity "czars" was Harold L. Ickes. The Petroleum Administration for War was established in December, 1942, with Ickes as administrator. Ickes was also aggressive, and since his major problem, the production of 100-octane gasoline, conflicted with the rubber program, the stage was set for a clash.

By the beginning of 1943, the President had designated four production programs as imperative. These were the escort vessel, aircraft, high-octane gasoline, and rubber programs. Unfortunately, these programs competed for the same materials and component parts, especially valves, boilers, heat exchangers, condensers, and electrical equipment, all of which were in short supply. It was impossible to complete each program during 1943, but the President had not indicated which program should take precedence. Nor had the Joint Chiefs of Staff made such a determination, although requested to do so by the WPB.

Nelson brought the matter before the Board at the meeting of the WPB on January 5, 1943. He stated that if the President or the Joint Chiefs determined which of the programs was to have precedence, the necessary orders would be issued. In the absence of such a determination, Nelson proposed to issue a directive establishing completion goals for facilities for the rubber and high-octane programs and for a portion of the escort vessel and aircraft programs. He stated that it must be recognized that the synthetic rubber program was in the "most hazardous position." Secretary of the Navy Frank Knox urged that all four programs be carried forward in balance and strongly objected to putting the rubber program in first position. Under Secretary of War Robert P. Patterson also objected to precedence for the rubber program, which he thought would result in serious loss to the high-octane and aircraft programs, and urged stringent conservation measures for rubber.[2] WPB then issued a directive scheduling the completion of plants for 55 per cent of the Buna S rubber program, which Nelson considered to be absolutely essential.

After that the battle was carried on in the press. On January 25, Jeffers charged that the Army and Navy and "loafers" were impeding the rubber program.[3] Elmer Davis, head of the Office of War Information, wrote Jeffers the next day rebuking him for violating the President's directive against the public airing of disputes, and charging him with contributing to "confusion at home" and to the "propaganda machines of our enemies." [4] Some time later Davis publicly charged Jeffers with trying to prevent the public from hearing the truth about the program.

Early in February the problem of the conflicting programs was aired before a House subcommittee, with Jeffers, Patterson, and James V. Forrestal testifying. After that came two months of relative peace.

The conflict flared up again when the newspapers of April 22 reported that Patterson, with the support of Ickes, maintained that the air attack would be slowed unless there was an increase in the production of 100-octane gasoline. Patterson stated that, in March, planes were grounded for lack of gas. The *New York Times* reported:

Directly responsible, according to both Mr. Patterson and Harold
Ickes, War Petroleum Administrator, is a competitive clash between
100-octane and synthetic rubber for certain vital scarce machinery.
Until now, synthetic rubber has held the inside track, so much so that
its expansion shortly will make it possible to "coddle" the civilian
public. . . .

In the Army and in some civilian circles there is resentment against
what military men call the "pity-the-poor-civilian" clique. Especially
they charge that William Jeffers, Rubber Administrator, has been so
intent on making a record in synthetic rubber that he has taken machinery needed both for combat gasoline and for escort ships . . .[5]

Jeffers replied in kind, calling the next day for an investigation, and it was reported that he said that either he or Patterson
would have to go. On April 23, the Truman Committee announced that it would investigate the matter, but the verbal
battle continued. The newspapers of April 25 quoted Jeffers as
suggesting that other officials might copy his methods of getting
a job done instead of "sitting around desks and issuing orders
and grousing." He also said, "You know, boys, this country
would be better off it some of us did more thinking and less
talking." [6] Presumably this latter advice was also meant for
other officials; Jeffers gave no indication of an intention to
follow it.

The Truman Committee opened its hearings on the matter on
April 27 with Nelson as the witness. Nelson stated his hope that
the investigation would substitute light for heat in the controversy, adding that "indulgence in such rivalries in time of war is
completely out of place." [7] He told the Senators that all of the
facts he would give them were already known to all of the
officials involved. Reminding them that Patterson's and Ickes'
charges of a gasoline shortage in March alleged that this was due
to his priority decision the previous December, Nelson pointed
out that it took from twelve to fifteen months from the projec-
tion of a high-octane plant to the production of its first gasoline

and that any current shortages resulted from decisions made at least a year before. He went on to explain that a major reason for a shortage of 100-octane gasoline was a very substantial underestimation of the amount that would be required and a failure to stockpile it before 1941, when it was readily available. Even as late as June, 1942, he said, the services' priority for high-octane gas and rubber was below that for other items of military equipment. He did not blame anyone for this, but said it was just one of the many failures to take advantage of the pre-war period to prepare.

Underlying the dispute was the continuing issue of how much was required to operate the civilian economy. Patterson had agreed to a relatively low priority for high-octane gas in June, when higher priorities were being assigned to items of military equipment. But the rubber program was for both the military and civilians, and he was certain that too much of it was going to end up in use by civilians; that they would be "coddled." This was an insoluble issue; no one *knew* how little the civilian economy could get by with. Nelson was certain that Patterson would have cut the rubber program well below the irreducible minimum needed by the civilian economy and was quite concerned about a breakdown in our transportation system if rubber were not available.

Nelson outlined his thinking to the Committee and the reasons for his decision to grant an overriding priority to 55 per cent of the rubber program. He hoped that closely balanced scheduling would keep the competing programs in balance from then on. He denied that there was an existing shortage of high-octane gasoline (although there was some maldistribution), but admitted that there would be a shortage in the future unless he was able to make up for the diversion of components to the rubber program.

Ickes followed Nelson on the morning of April 28, 1943.

After citing the achievements of the Petroleum Administration for War in accelerating production of 100-octane gasoline and asserting that he had always raised the orders given him, he said it had all been accomplished in spite of "a really baffling lack of understanding by many persons in high authority of the vital essentiality of 100-octane." [8] Although Ickes extolled PAW accomplishments in getting greater production of high-octane gas from existing facilities, the general import of his statement was that the 100-octane program should be given an immediate overriding priority and that the priority of the rubber program should be downgraded.

Under questioning by Senator Ball the insoluble nature of the problem was brought out:

Senator Ball. Is there any way from here on that you can speed up bringing these new facilities into production without coming into conflict with other programs, escort vessels, and rubber, both of which I think we would agree are very critical?

Secretary Ickes. We would come in conflict with the rubber program and we would probably come into conflict, at least to some extent, with the Navy program and the Maritime Commission program.

Senator Ball. Then isn't it a question that all of those programs are urgent; you can't win the war without escort vessels?

Secretary Ickes. That is right. It is a question of relative essentiality.

Senator Ball. We don't want to get down below the level on rubber. Isn't it, then, a question that some agency has to decide how the critical components that go into all these programs are divided up to get the best balanced picture all the way down the line?

Secretary Ickes. That is right, but we have never subscribed to the belief that we have been in balance, in proper balance, since the January decision.[9]

A few moments later the question came up again:

Senator Brewster. You do recognize, Mr. Secretary, the need of some other things than oil and gasoline in order to win the war.

Secretary Ickes. Yes, but I say again, without aviation gasoline we aren't going to win the war.

Senator Brewster. And that could also be said of rubber.

Secretary Ickes. Well, a certain amount. The Army ought to have all the rubber it needs—

Senator Brewster (interposing). Yes.

Secretary Ickes. But it doesn't mean that 100-octane gasoline should be postponed for further increases in nonessential civilian use of rubber.

Senator Brewster. I am sure we all agree with that, and the general impression in the country is that the reason there is nonessential use of rubber is that they are allowed to use gasoline . . .[10]

Ickes agreed with this observation. No one reminded him that rationing of gasoline would have been instituted several months sooner if he had not talked the President out of doing so on the grounds that it was not needed.

All in all, Ickes unwittingly strengthened Nelson's position by demonstrating the tendency of the "czars" to measure the war effort by their own programs, underlining the need for someone to make the over-all decisions.

That afternoon Forrestal presented the Navy position. His remarks contrasted sharply with those of the other protagonists. He began by saying:

The Navy doesn't assume any position in these hearings except the very simple statement that its own responsibility is the pushing of its construction of fighting ships and auxiliaries with all of its ability and with the greatest possible speed. At the same time, it recognizes that there are a number of other segments of the war program which have great importance, and while the Navy might accelerate some of its own objectives by the use of what I call pressure methods . . . it has never used those methods because it doesn't believe in them, and it doesn't intend to do so now because of its firm conviction that you cannot run this vast and intricate war program in any other than an orderly manner and on an orderly and not disorderly foundation. . . .

The Navy is also fully aware of the imperative need for the maintenance of that part of the civilian economy essential to the war. It does not need to be reminded that the workers in its plants need automobiles to get to work. . . .

The Navy does not assume to itself any broader understanding of the complexities of our economy than that possessed by its associates in the war effort. By that I mean that we don't offer . . . we don't possess or pose as having any greater wisdom than our associates, and these remarks do not mean to imply that we alone have the answer. We know we haven't. There is, however, one reason why the Navy is at least as conscious as anybody else, and possibly a little more so, of the necessity of balance in the program. The reason is this: We have many programs that must go forward simultaneously, and in order to fight a successful war those efforts must be prosecuted vigorously as a whole. There is a great temptation even within the Navy to lift out one particular segment of a program and to let it override everything else to meet an immediate emergency.[11]

Forrestal went on to say that Navy experience had convinced them that it was unwise to grant overriding priorities to any program. Although he discussed the urgency of the escort vessel program, he maintained that all the "must" programs should be kept in balance by careful scheduling. He objected to the method used in stepping up the rubber program, that is, the overriding directive, but he was careful to refrain from attaching blame to anyone for the vigor with which the rubber and 100-octane programs were being prosecuted. Forrestal practiced what he preached; there was great temptation to ask for an overriding directive for escort vessels, but he did not. He indicated that he thought the scheduling being worked out by Wilson and his assistant, Ralph J. Cordiner, in the WPB could solve the problems of balance, and he recommended to the Committee members that they give these efforts their support.

Patterson testified on May 3. He was somewhat restrained in comparison with his press statements, but he argued strongly that the 100-octane gas program was the critical program at that time, that it had been badly hurt by the rubber directive, and that it needed greater emphasis and a higher priority. He summed up his position thus:

> The synthetic rubber program is an important program. I do not believe, however, that today it is as urgent a program for war purposes as the 100-octane gasoline program. And there are other important programs, of course, including escort vessels and merchant shipping.
>
> But there is every indication that the rubber situation is in much better condition than 100-octane gasoline. I take it that the recent relaxation of restrictions placed on the use of rubber would not have come about if the rubber outlook had not improved to the point that any crisis in the supply of rubber has been passed. From present indications there will be rubber but not enough 100-octane gasoline.[12]

Patterson told the Committee that he and Jeffers had met and were planning a trip together to look over the situation. This did not enable him to escape a lecture from Senator Brewster.

Senator Brewster. Were you given ample opportunity to present your problem from time to time to the authority that had the final word?

Mr. Patterson. Yes, sir.

Senator Brewster. So you did argue your case from time to time.

Mr. Patterson. Yes, sir. I went on a trip some three or four weeks ago . . . and I saw the conditions in regard to fuel and was told by the commanding officers of the curtailments in training that had been necessitated by the limited supplies they were given. I brought the facts to the attention of the Petroleum Board at that time on my return, at which representatives of the War Production Board were present. . . . I believe that the discussion of the matter, the public awareness of this situation, will result in a redoubling of the efforts of the petroleum industry . . . and also in the thorough cooperation of all governmental agencies concerned in this problem.

Senator Brewster. This was, you say, some three to four weeks ago that you made this trip?

Mr. Patterson. Yes, sir.

Senator Brewster. And you presented your findings on your return to the agencies involved?

Mr. Patterson. Yes, sir.

Senator Brewster. Your statement to the press must have been issued rather promptly after that.

Mr. Patterson. Some days after; yes, sir.

Senator Brewster. Did you have any intimation as to any lack of sympathetic or intelligent approach to the reconsideration of the program which you were then urging?

Mr. Patterson. Of course, there was a good deal of sympathy shown, but it seemed to me that stronger measures were necessary than the signs I saw were already being taken.

Senator Brewster. You have been a judge, have you not?

Mr. Patterson. Yes, sir; some ten years, and that was quite a long time ago.

Senator Brewster. And you have recognized the need of the court having at least a little time to consider, have you not?

Mr. Patterson. Yes, sir.

Senator Brewster. You didn't care particularly about the attorney's appealing to the people while the court was considering the case, did you?

Mr. Patterson. They used to do it a good deal.

Senator Brewster. I am sure not with the approval of the court.

Mr. Patterson. No.[13]

And Brewster added a parting shot a little later:

Senator Brewster. You indicated, Judge Patterson, a certain degree of satisfaction with the results of your explosion, if I may so term it, on this subject. It had focused attention. Do you feel that we can run a war quite in that way?

Mr. Patterson. No.[14]

The Committee agreed with Patterson that we had to get the gasoline as well as the rubber, but some doubt was expressed that another overriding directive was the way to do it.

Jeffers concluded the list of witnesses the next day. He, too, was more restrained than in his press conference, but claimed that apparently the only complaint against him was that he had done his job too well. He not only argued that the rubber program had not hurt any of the other programs but that "the momentum of the rubber program has dragged forward all of these phases of the war." [15] He explained that the President had directed him to follow the recommendations of the Baruch report on rubber, which had urged top priority for the rubber program. It was clear from his testimony that his definition of essential civilian needs was much broader than Patterson's, and probably broader than Nelson's, but he was able to answer the statement of Patterson's about relaxation of restrictions. Patterson had referred to an order permitting unlimited recapping of tires. This was done with reclaimed rubber, which was not usable for military purposes. The Committee did not question this, but did question the wisdom of not establishing a priority for essential users, since supplies of camelback (an essential ingredient) were not adequate for unlimited recapping although the supply of reclaimed rubber was. There was little cross-examination, but it was suggested to Jeffers that there were better ways of settling these problems than the method he and Patterson had been using.

The Committee also held private hearings with these men, since much of the data on which their positions were based could not be made public for security reasons. Before the Committee could prepare a report, Nelson discussed the issue with the President, who upheld Nelson's decision. In July, Nelson reluctantly raised the priority of the 100-octane gasoline program. By this time the rubber program was in relatively good shape.

The Committee's report was presented to the Senate on May 6, 1943. Taking no position on the merits of the issue, the report began: "The conflict between the synthetic rubber, aviation-gasoline, and escort-vessel programs has been relieved and largely removed by bringing the respective loyal, competent, and aggressive disputants face to face. This should have occurred

days ago in the ordinary quiet process of administration." [16]
The report reviewed the events leading up to the hearings and
noted that the public, which the disputants had invited to judge
the issue, could not have all the facts on which to make a judgment. It pointed out that the central problem was one of coordination and control:

> The task of control and guidance is of utmost importance. Clear
> leadership in strong hands is required. The influence from above
> must be always towards unity. Where necessary, heads must be
> knocked together.[17]

The report then continued with a discussion of the difficulties
of the War Production Board, its failure to exercise the powers
vested in it, the dilution of its authority by the creation of
"czars" who weakened WPB but lacked the power to determine
the whole program themselves. It commented, "the lines of
authority are confusing even on paper. As a practical matter they
breed disputes such as that under consideration." The Committee recommended that (1) the strong over-all authority of WPB
"be made a living reality" and (2) "without dilution of the power
of the Chairman, the War Production Board should function as
a board," where the persons in charge of the major war program
could sit down and discuss and work out their problems.[18]

As has been noted in the previous chapter, this report was a
factor in the establishment of the Office of War Mobilization as
a coordinating agency. OWM provided a place where disputes
of this kind could be settled before it became necessary for a
Congressional committee to step in and try to settle them.

CONCLUSION

Even in retrospect it is difficult to pass judgment on the merits
of the issue. Forrestal presented the ideal in his argument against
the use of overriding priorities on any program and for the
orderly scheduling of balanced production of all imperative pro-

grams. But perhaps the synthetic rubber program had been let go for so long that the steps taken were absolutely necessary to prevent an impairment of the economy that would have been worse than the dislocation caused by the rubber directive. It does seem to be true that the problem in 100-octane gasoline at the time was a potential rather than an existing shortage. Given this fact and the immediacy of the need for rubber, it was almost inevitable that the method of the overriding priority was adopted. That this method (which was used to solve other critical shortages) did not bring the dire consequences its opponents foresaw is probably due to the fantastic productivity and responsiveness of the American economy when unlimited funds are poured into it. The United States succeeded in meeting a series of critical shortages of materials and products by borrowing from future production of other critical items, yet by the end of 1943 most of the "debts" had been repaid and a rough balance had been achieved among the vital production programs.

Nevertheless, the Truman Committee performed a useful service in bringing Patterson, Ickes, and Jeffers together to settle their public argument. Rudolph Halley believed this to be an example of the Committee's best work.[19] Apparently he thought that the Committee's most useful work was in coordinating the scattered war agencies during the period when there was no effective administrative agency to perform this vital function. It is true that before the creation of the Office of War Mobilization the Committee did perform some of the functions of a coordinating agency. This was not by virtue of any administrative decision-making power vested in it, however, but by its putting pressure on administrative officials to come to decisions and stick by them, or, as in this case, by backing up the War Production Board, which did have responsibility for coordination. In this dispute Nelson had made the decision; he was having difficulty making it stick until the Truman Committee (and then the President) came to his support.

Settling interagency disputes and coordinating the efforts of different agencies engaged in the same great endeavor are part of the broader problem of organization. These matters are not properly within the province of a Congressional committee, especially one without legislative powers. Nor can a Congressional committee deal effectively with problems of organization and coordination. About all the Truman Committee could do was call attention to the problems and keep the spotlight on them until there was some effort at solution. This it did. The Committee was convinced that there should be a strong agency in control of the war effort, directed by one man who had the power to enforce his decisions on all agencies. The Committee repeatedly called attention to the shortcomings of the Office of Production Management in this respect, and its vigorous condemnation of OPM in the First Annual Report was certainly a factor in at least the timing of the establishment of the War Production Board. And the Committee constantly prodded Nelson to exercise the powers he had been given.

The public dispute over conflicting war programs resulted in increased Congressional support for the establishment of a War Mobilization Board. When Roosevelt blocked this move by the creation of the Office of War Mobilization, the Truman Committee was satisfied that the major organizational need of the war effort had been met. Less than a month after OWM was created, Truman announced that the Committee and Byrnes had agreed that the Committee would "from time to time on its initiative submit to Mr. Byrnes conflicts of authority and cases of waste or inefficient administration which the Committee believes can best be corrected through action by Mr. Byrnes." [20] In other words, the Committee formally recognized Byrnes as the coordinator. Actually, the Committee's expectations for OWM went beyond that. The Truman Committee expected that Byrnes would take over active and direct control of the domestic side of the war effort. In spite of his unquestioned power to do so, Byrnes did not, for he wished to confine his role to the necessary minimum of coordination required to keep the sprawling war organization functioning. The Committee became increasingly critical of Byrnes for his failure to take over active direction of the war effort, although most of this criticism came after Truman had left the Committee.

The Truman Committee's extended efforts to get centralized control and direction of the domestic side of the war effort were in marked contrast to the more prevalent tendency of Congress to divide and splinter authority and to weaken the executive branch of the government. The Committee must have known that success in this endeavor would decrease its own influence, which indeed creation of the Office of War Mobilization did. But there is no evidence that the Committee's persistence on this issue stemmed from any clearly held theory of administration. The Committee's attitude seems to have come from its deep concern with conflicts between military and civilian needs. The Committee was more concerned with this problem than was Congress as a whole and was much less willing to accept military judgments on matters beyond strategy and tactics. This was probably due as much to its intimate contact with the issues between the military and civilian spheres as to accidents of Committee and staff membership. Even on the issue of civilian control of the military there is little evidence that the Committee adopted any theory beyond the firm belief that there must be "civilian control."

Rather, the Truman Committee's insistence on centralized direction of the war effort seems to have been based on the feeling that if open conflicts were permitted to develop between the military and civilian agencies, the military would usually win.

This feeling was not without justification. The Committee wanted effective direction of the war effort to force the military to consider the needs of the civilian economy, and it wanted a coordinating agency strong enough to withstand pressures from single-minded agencies. In short, it wanted balanced production, and its efforts contributed to achieving a closer approximation of this goal.

5) The Committee and the Military: The Canol Project

The General [Somervell] did not know much about oil, but he thought they had made the greatest discovery in recent years. I never did learn why it didn't work, but it didn't.

Admiral William D. Leahy [1]

THE PROJECT

In 1941, Dr. Vilhjalmur Stefansson, the explorer, made a suggestion to the War Department concerning the development of a supply route through Canada to Alaska. Subsequently, there were extended discussions with respect to several possible routes for a highway or railroad for this purpose, but no decision was made. After Pearl Harbor there was renewed interest in the project, and Lieutenant General Brehon B. Somervell asked James H. Graham to get him the information on which to act. Graham was dean of the Engineering School of the University of Kentucky, serving as a technical advisor to Somervell on a dollar-a-year basis. He participated in further discussions of the proposed highway or railroad and the possible routes. The idea of a railroad was abandoned, but the Alcan Highway project was approved and constructed. Graham played no direct role in the decision.

Dr. Stefansson had suggested a route which went by Norman Wells, where Imperial Oil, Ltd., a Canadian subsidiary of Standard Oil Company of New Jersey, operated a small oil project which might provide limited amounts of fuel. This route was rejected, but the idea of an oil supply closer to Alaska than the United States took root. Graham apparently considered the idea during February and March of 1942 and discussed it casually with one or two military friends, but he engaged in no systematic consultation as to the feasibility of the project. In April, Major General Arthur H. Carter, Chief of the Fiscal Division of the Services of Supply, contacted Jersey Standard for Graham and asked that qualified persons from Imperial Oil be sent to Washington to discuss the Norman Wells operation. Accordingly, two representatives of Imperial and one from Standard Oil met with Graham on April 29, 1942. Also present were Carter, Air Force Major General St. Clair Streett, and General Walter B. Pryon, a former vice-president of Gulf Oil Corporation then with the Army Services of Supply. The representatives of Imperial Oil told the group that the company had taken small amounts of crude oil from its field at Norman Wells for many years, operating only in the summer. The crude was processed on the spot for local consumption. They said that with more holes it might be possible to get a yield of as high as 3,000 barrels per day but were not particularly optimistic.[2] General Pryon made two contributions to the discussion: He agreed that there was a possibility of getting 3,000 barrels a day from the project, and he answered a question from Graham to the effect that a four-inch pipeline would carry 3,000 barrels a day. General Streett, for his part, told the group that it would be a "godsend" to have a local supply of high-octane gasoline for the Alcan Highway and the string of airfields being established along that road.[3] It was an informal meeting in which there was a general discussion of the project, but essentially Graham obtained only two items of information from it, the need and the possible supply.

After the meeting Graham prepared a memorandum for General Somervell, recommending—

1. Drilling more wells in the Norman field to increase production by September, 1942.

2. Surveying and constructing a four-inch pipeline from Norman to Whitehorse, in the Yukon, to be in operation by September 15, 1942.

3. Finding suitable refining equipment in the United States and dismantling, transporting, and erecting it at Whitehorse, ready for October 1, 1942.

4. Action to provide for the transportation of materials and equipment for the operation.[4]

No reasons or supporting evidence of any kind were included in the memorandum; it was a set of bare recommendations as simple as though he had recommended: "Build a bridge from New York to London" (and in view of the specified schedule, almost as fantastic). Somervell approved the memorandum the same day and the next day directed the Chief of Engineers to take the necessary steps to carry out the recommendations.[5]

The considerations behind the decision were the threat to Alaska from the Japanese and the fear that shipping could not be relied upon to get fuel to Alaska for its defense. It was planned to defend Alaska primarily by air power, and ferrying of planes to Russia was being carried out through Alaska; both required high-octane gasoline in substantial quantities. The most important reason given later, however, was the fear that the Navy could not ensure the safe shipment of gasoline up the west coast of Canada, even through the inland waterway. Lesser considerations were the certain shortages of petroleum and tankers in which to ship it. The use of barges through the inland waterway was not considered.

With all possible allowance for these considerations, the decision still seems unbelievably casual. Although the pipeline was to extend about 550 miles from Norman to Whitehorse over unsurveyed (some of it unmapped) territory, much of which was muskeg (mossy bogs), and would have to cross two mountain ranges, no effort was made to determine how difficult the job would be or what specific conditions would be met—factors that would deeply affect the vital consideration of time. Graham did not even consult Dr. Stefansson! Nor were the Army Engineers, who had to do the job, consulted. No estimate of the time required to complete the project was obtained from any informed source. Graham apparently picked his target dates because they marked the end of the summer and such work had to be done seasonally in that territory (Norman is close to the Arctic Circle).

No effort was made to determine the amounts of materials, manpower, and shipping that would be required to complete the project, or the amount of shipping that would be required to transport men and materials to the Yukon. Neither the Petroleum Coordinator for War, Harold L. Ickes, nor the War Production Board was consulted to determine if the same amount of manpower and materials could be used more effectively somewhere else. The Navy was not consulted as to whether it could protect shipping to Alaska, although this was presumably the major consideration behind the project. Later, Graham repeatedly told the Truman Committee, "I don't regard cost in time of war." He did not seem to understand that cost merely represented materials and manpower (plus waste, as Fulton kept reminding him).[6]

Two other items in the memorandum deserve comment. Four-inch pipe was decided upon just as casually as the rest of the project. It was known to be available, and it would carry 3,000 barrels a day. The Army's technical advisors later informed it that the use of six-inch pipe would reduce the number of pumping stations from twelve to two, with a use of only 20 per cent more steel. Since pumping equipment was one of the scarcer items throughout the war, six-inch pipe was used for the western 100 miles of the line, eliminating two pumping stations.

Both Norman and Whitehorse were in Canadian territory. Fairbanks, Alaska was an alternative location for the refinery, and Dr. Stefansson had originally suggested it as the location. There was a case for both locations, and apparently Whitehorse was chosen because it was located about in the middle of the Alcan Highway. Miles H. Knowles, who was the Army representative with the Truman Committee when it visited the Canol Project, later said that Fairbanks was not chosen because it was in American territory and the project would then have come under Ickes' jurisdiction.[7]

Graham could afford to be casual, for he was not responsible. Somervell was. It is difficult to understand the offhand manner in which he made such a far-reaching decision. He knew that Graham had no special knowledge of petroleum engineering or of conditions in the Yukon. He knew that the conditions were extremely difficult, but he did not consult his engineers, either. The only excuse for making the decision without further investigation was the need for utilizing the summer if the project were to be completed on schedule. But Somervell later testified that he knew that the project could not be completed by fall, 1942, and expected that it could be by the summer of 1943.[8] Somervell had no concern for costs; but he must have realized that dollars represented scarce manpower and materials. It is reasonable to suppose that the decision was made, in a manner that Somervell would never have tolerated in a subordinate, in large part because it appealed to his imagination. He was very proud of his famous slogan, "The difficult we do immediately, the impossible takes a little longer," and it seems fair to conclude that the "impossible" had more appeal to him than the easy.[9]

In the spring of 1942 there was sufficient reason to investigate the possibility of developing a source of petroleum in the Yukon. There may even have been some justification for directing the work to begin. There was none for continuing it without a thorough reconsideration after the views of others were made known to the Army Service Forces.

Graham's memorandum was circulated to all the persons present at the April 29 meeting. When it was received by the Imperial Oil Company, a vice-president, R. V. Le Sueur, in consultation with the Imperial representatives at the meeting, sent a letter to General Carter on May 2. The letter expressed grave doubt as to the feasibility of the pipeline project and suggested using cargo planes instead to provide the necessary fuel.[10] Its contents were known to Somervell. On April 30, the Imperial representatives met with Major General T. M. Robins, deputy Chief of Engineers, and expressed some reluctance to get involved with the project. Robins commented that "ten times the volume of deliveries contemplated by the pipe line could be made by barges already available from inland United States rivers, and at one-tenth of the cost and effort." [11] But he added that he would do the job he had been ordered to do. He did not communicate his views to Somervell, nor was he ever asked. Although it was an offhand remark, it turned out to be a reasonable prediction.

The Army hired the Standard Oil Company of California as technical consultant on the project and to operate the pipeline and refinery. On June 4, 1942, J. L. Hanna of that company wrote to Secretary of War Henry L. Stimson that the pipeline could not be constructed in the time scheduled and that the yield in high-octane gas when completed would be quite small. As consultant, California Standard recommended instead the immediate construction of dispersed storage facilities, which could be constructed at much less cost in time, materials, and manpower, and which would be safer against attack.[12]

Early in May, Ickes found out about the project through his deputy, Ralph K. Davies, formerly vice-president of California Standard, who had heard of it in casual conversation. Ickes wrote to Patterson inquiring about the project, and Patterson confirmed it. On June 3, Ickes wrote to Henry L. Stimson, expressing regret that the Office of Petroleum Coordinator for War had not been consulted. He agreed with the Army's objective but doubted that its means were the most desirable. Ickes noted the difficulties in construction and operation of the pipeline and the lack of available facilities for making high-octane gasoline. He suggested a storage project and a pipeline to distribute petroleum products brought up the coast to Skagway by ship, and pointed out that "one average-size tanker could in four trips supply as much aviation fuel as could be manufactured in this proposed 3,000-barrel refinery during the year," assuming maximum production.[13] Patterson replied, expressing regret that Ickes had not been consulted but telling him that the project was well under way and that it was the desire of the War Department to complete the project.

Ickes wrote to Stimson again on June 22, pointing out that it would be late in 1943, at the earliest, before the project would produce any significant supply of aviation gasoline and again urging the storage project as a means of getting larger quantities of gasoline there sooner. On July 7, he received a letter from Stimson saying that the suggestion for a distribution pipeline (which California Standard Oil had also recommended) was being adopted. This was done and was never criticized, for it had some real military value. Stimson told Ickes that commitments were being deferred pending the results of further drilling in the Norman area. Stimson also accepted Ickes' offer to send a geologist up to Norman to study the project, and Ickes sent

Glen F. Ruby, former chief geologist of the Hudson's Bay Company.

On September 5, Ickes was informed by Patterson that "several new wells have indicated production possibilities sufficient to justify resumption of the original project" and that the Army was proceeding with the project. Ickes tried unsuccessfully to get action suspended until the Ruby report was submitted. This report was transmitted to the Secretary of War on November 29. On the basis of the report Ickes concluded that the pipeline and refinery was not justifiable, "even as an emergency project," although both he and Ruby recommended continued exploration of the area for further oil deposits.[14] Patterson replied that since 3,000 barrels of crude were assured, the project was fully justified.

On May 6, 1942, an item of $25,000,000 was added to the War Department budget for the fiscal year 1943, for the construction of military facilities from Norman to Whitehorse. No other description was given in the budget request, although the Budget Bureau was given a general description orally. In February, 1943, Budget Bureau examiners learned that the estimated cost of the project had risen to $85,000,000, plus $10,000,000 for further oil prospecting in the area. Although the War Department had great freedom in selecting undertakings without prior justification to the Budget Bureau, it was decided in the Bureau to conduct a field inspection. For this purpose Robert W. Coghill, a petroleum consultant, was sent to the area after he had studied what was known of the project in Washington. He was accompanied by the Bureau examiner who normally handled Corps of Engineers estimates. On June 2, 1943, the Budget Bureau sent copies of the reports of these men to the Secretary of War. The accompanying letter noted that 1943 obligations would amount to $65,300,000 and that another

$53,780,000 would be required in 1944, a total of $119,080,000. The Bureau recommended at least a cutback in the project:

The extreme solutions to the problem seem to be, on the one hand, to carry forward the program as planned, and, on the other, to stop the entire project and supply the same quantity of gasoline by seven tanker loads a year moving along the inner water passage from the south to the Skagway pipeline. Perhaps the proper answer lies between the two.[15]

The two investigators had recommended the abandonment of the Norman-Whitehorse pipeline and the refinery unless they were vital to the war. Since the conditions had changed and neither the west coast of North America nor Alaska were in danger, the Budget Bureau wished the Joint Chiefs of Staff to review the project to determine if it was still considered vital. It might be noted at this point that the Budget Bureau had received a letter from California Standard Oil Company early in April stating that nothing had occurred to change its earlier opinion that the storage plan was superior to the Canol Project.[16]

Copies of the Budget Bureau letter to the Secretary of War were sent to the Chairman of the War Production Board and the Petroleum Administrator for War. Ickes replied promptly, stressing his long-standing concern over the project. This letter was passed on to Stimson. On July 27, Robert P. Patterson replied that eliminating part of the refinery and other economies would reduce the total cost to $88,000,000. Abandoning the project would result in the loss of the $50,000,000 already spent. He concluded, "Military necessity requires that the Canol Project be completed as rapidly as possible." [17] Before an attempt to get the principals together for further discussion of the project had succeeded, War Mobilization Director Byrnes ordered a review of the undertaking.

The War Production Board was also interested in the project. The War Department never took up the subject with the WPB, but the Board inadvertently heard of it in the fall of 1942. In a letter to the procurement agencies in December discussing WPB attempts to curtail construction, Fred Searls, Jr., Director of the WPB Facilities Bureau, mentioned the project in Alaska. He noted that strategic considerations apparently were involved and asked for views as to WPB review of the project.[18] Patterson replied immediately, stating that the projects were undertaken for strategic reasons. Searls made a few inquiries and, discussing also the Alcan Highway, replied in part:

> Such inquiries have, of course, been of a guarded nature but have served to confirm my own opinion that the entire program will subtract from, rather than add to, the war effort.
> Judge Patterson's letter . . . confirms the statement . . . that the Alaskan developments under construction have been undertaken basically for "strategic reasons." This infers that reliance must be placed on the facilities being projected, under certain possible contingencies. If, as a matter of fact, physical conditions are such that reliance cannot be placed on the facilities, then the "strategic reasons" are unsound, and it follows that experienced civilian opinion and comment are entitled to be heard—even though persons making the comment have not been acquainted with the details of the military thought, and, planning for utilization of the facilities. . . . If, in fact, the expenditure of materials, equipment, and manpower that are necessarily included in this program which will cost in excess of $200,000,000, will lead to the establishment of a line of communication which will be unusable, then it does not matter whether the intention is to provide an emergency route to Asia or to the Alaska Peninsula, and it does become a matter of concern to other agencies competing for the materials and manpower involved, as to whether the program is feasible within reasonable conceptions of the duration of the war.

After reviewing the reasons for probable failure of the projects, Searls concluded:

> It is urgently recommended that this entire program be submitted to the Requirements Committee of the War Production Board. It is

not a secret program for it has been subject to comment in various published articles, and will receive additional publicity, not all of which will be as favorable as that which has so far appeared. It is pretty certain to be investigated by Congress. If it is a failure, as is freely predicted in this letter, the public criticism will attach not only to the Army but to the War Production Board, which has never passed on the project.

If the Army has sound reasons for defending the program, there should be no reluctance to presenting it to the Requirements Committee which can, if necessary, hold a secret session for the purpose.

If this is not done, it is the writer's opinion that a record is left that the War Production Board stopped hundreds of useful, though not essential, civilian projects to save material, only to have it used for a huge and useless program in Alaska, of which it has never had official cognizance, and which will never serve a useful purpose.[19]

Patterson replied that "the War Department by no means concedes that a project of this nature . . . is a project which the War Department is called upon to explain or justify to the Requirements Committee of the Facilities Board." [20] Having put his position on the record, Searls dropped the matter.

In March, 1943, Nelson requested H. LeRoy Whitney, as technical consultant, to undertake a study of the whole Alaskan construction program. Whitney, after an extensive study, reported to Nelson that "it is both our right and our duty to insist that the present wastage of scarce materials and equipment be immediately stopped" and recommended that Nelson and Ickes take steps to that end.[21] Before anything was accomplished, both the Budget Bureau and the Truman Committee were involved with the issue.

THE INVESTIGATION

The Truman Committee began investigating the Canol Project in the summer of 1943. In September a subcommittee visited the Yukon and held private hearings. Knowles went there with the subcommittee as the War Department representative and conducted his own investigation. On his return to Washington he informed Julius H. Amberg, Assistant to the Secretary of War, that the Canol Project was indefensible.[22] After that Amberg handled the case.

In October the Joint Chiefs of Staff, at Byrnes's request, considered the project. After the Budget Bureau reports, Somervell prepared a memorandum for the Joint Chiefs on the case for continuing the project. Essentially the case rested on the need for oil, the fact that construction was well under way and would produce oil before any other project, and the statement that completion of the project would "affect material savings in critical transportation facilities." [23] This memorandum was misleading in three respects: (1) it stated that an intensive study had been made of the Norman Wells field before the project was started, (2) it quoted Ickes on the necessity for developing new sources of oil but did not mention that he was actively opposed to this project on the grounds that more oil could be produced elsewhere at a smaller cost in material and manpower, and (3) the computation of shipping savings on which it was based used the volume of crude produced at Norman as a basis of comparison rather than the volume of refined products, which was one-third smaller. The Truman Committee later questioned him sharply on all three points.

The Joint Chiefs of Staff reviewed the matter on October 26, 1943, and decided that the completion of the project was "necessary to the war effort." They refused to give Senator Truman any reason for this decision (this was not unusual, however). The Joint Chiefs actually gave the matter little consideration, although this was the only time during the war that the matter came before them. A newly established agency of the Joint Chiefs, the Joint Production Survey Committee, made the recommendations after a study, in cooperation with the Army-Navy Petroleum Board, that included hearings at which a representative of the Petroleum Administration for War appeared. Apparently, no one else who was opposed to continuation was heard. The Joint Production Survey Committee recommended completion, and the Joint Chiefs accepted this recommendation without examining the evidence on which it was based.[24] This action was taken exactly three weeks after the Joint Chiefs ordered a reduction in the size of the force stationed in Alaska. The decision accomplished two things: (1) it effected a sharing of the responsibility and (2) it made it virtually impossible for civilian agencies or Congress to question the decision.

In November a subcommittee of the Truman Committee consisting of Senators Kilgore and Ferguson held a number of private hearings at which the facts in the case were developed.[25] On November 22, the full Committee began public hearings in which the facts were put on record. On December 2, 1943, Senator Truman wrote to the Secretary of the Navy (Frank Knox), the Secretary of War (Stimson), the Petroleum Administrator for War (Ickes), and the Chairman of the War Production Board (Nelson), urging them to hold a meeting to decide the disposition of the Canol Project. The meeting was held on December 9. Nelson, Ickes, and Knox agreed that the project should be abandoned to save the $30,000,000 remaining unspent. Stimson disagreed and wrote to Truman explaining his reasons. He thought that the actual saving would only amount to $10,000,000, that the oil in the field would be valuable, and that since the military leaders had determined upon its necessity, it should be continued. Actually, $28,650,000 more was spent on the project, although not all of this would have been saved by abandoning it in December of 1943.[26]

On November 23, at his request, Patterson appeared before the Truman Committee to defend the project—and not only defend it but praise it. He began by saying:

The War Department is proud of Canol. . . . Canol was a bold undertaking. The results so far have surpassed our hopes. We are confident that even greater success lies ahead. . . .

We uncovered a rich continental resource of oil, far beyond the original target of 3,000 barrels a day. Twenty thousand barrels a day is now assured. We already have uncovered an estimated pool of 50 to 100 million barrels. That is a major oil field in anybody's language. . . .[27]

The prospecting financed by the Army had uncovered greater oil reserves than had been anticipated. However, Imperial Oil estimated them at 35 million barrels, and 7,500 barrels a day was the maximum rate of production ever achieved. And the 3,000 barrels-a-day pipeline was not expected to be completed before March or April of 1944.

The cross-examination was brutal. Patterson fell back to the defense that the Joint Chiefs had declared the project necessary and that any supply at the source was valuable. Senator Kilgore questioned him vigorously about the fact that 3,000 barrels a day were expected to produce only 479 barrels of 100-octane gasoline (plus about 1500 barrels of other products), and this exchange took place:

Senator Kilgore. . . . I am wondering really how much of an aid that aviation gasoline would be to the strategy of defending Alaska with an all-out defense at that time.

Mr. Patterson. Any supply you could get at the source—what are you laughing at, Mr. Fulton?

Mr. Fulton. No matter.

Mr. Patterson. You have been laughing all through this. I haven't seen the humor in it yet.

Mr. Fulton. I have been laughing at the concept that any supply, no matter what it was, would be valuable, without regard to the cost in man-hours and materials together.[28]

Somervell appeared before the Committee on December 20. He made an able presentation of his case for the project, but the cross-examination forced him into much the same position as that of Patterson—defending the project on the basis of local source and the determination of its military necessity by the Joint Chiefs. He was now much more cautious about the value of the project, defending it primarily in terms of the necessity in 1942 and admitting at one point that he probably would not have approved it if he had known it would not be completed before 1944.[29] Senator Connally did his best to protect both Patterson and Somervell while they were testifying, but the Army position was untenable.

On January 8, 1944, the Truman Committee reported to the Senate on the Canol Project. The report cited the facts of the case and reached a number of conclusions, including:

1. The project was undertaken without adequate study, Somervell's information being deficient in these respects: (a) there was inadequate technical knowledge of the Norman field, (b) there was no estimate of costs, "which reflect use of critical materials and manpower," (c) the date of completion "was on its face impossible of accomplishment," and (d) there was "no consideration of possible alternative methods of obtaining the same or greater supplies of oil." No consideration at all was given any of these factors except the first.

2. The time before April 30, 1942, was not utilized to make an adequate study.

3. The Army was quickly warned of the "unsoundness and excessive cost" of the project by qualified persons. "There may be some slight excuse for General Somervell's original hasty decision in view of the tremendous pressure on him at the time, but his continued insistence on the project in the face of these repeated warnings is inexcusable."

4. Instead of making a contribution to the war effort, the project was a drain on our resources during 1942 and 1943.[30]

The Committee did not make a recommendation as to continuing the project:

> *The committee is definitely of the opinion that the Canol Project should not have been undertaken, and that it should have been abandoned when the difficulties were called to the attention of the War Department.* Projects of this character ought to be undertaken only at the direction and with the approval of the Petroleum Administration for War. However, this project was undertaken by the War Department and has been so largely completed that only a small amount, proportionately, could be saved by abandoning it now. The committee therefore believes that the decision as to whether it should be abandoned now should be made by the War Department.[31]

In order to continue the project, the Army Service Forces had to secure further funds from Congress. An attempt was made to bury the request for funds for the Canol Project in the funds allotted to the Northwest Service Command. The War Department appropriation bill for the fiscal year 1945 contained an item of about $1,800,000,000 for the Corps of Engineers, with no specification as to its use. Even the ten volumes of accompanying detail contained only a one-line item of $34,-250,000 for the Northwest Service Command, marked "secret." There was no mention of the Canol Project anywhere.[32]

Fulton had warned Senator Truman, who was a member of the military subcommittee of the Appropriations Committee, to watch for the Canol Project request. Under pressure from the military subcommittee and the Truman Committee, it was admitted that the request for the Northwest Service Command contained items totaling $16,439,688 for the operation and maintenance of the Canol Project, of which $12,132,460 was for the pipeline and refinery operation. Fulton then demanded of the War Department an estimate of the fiscal year 1945 and a statement of the cost of procuring a like quantity of products from other sources. Amberg informed Fulton that these products could be obtained and sent from the United States to Skagway for $2,568,997, or from Aruba in the West Indies for $3,267,-893.[33] The Petroleum Administration for War informed Fulton that shipping was available for the supply involved.

On June 21, 1944, when the Senate was considering the War Department appropriation bill for fiscal year 1945, Senator Ferguson informed the Senate of these facts. But he said he would not offer an amendment to delete the request, and continued:

I understand that the Joint Chiefs of Staff have assumed responsibility for handling the funds, and I do not desire in any way to preclude them from obtaining what they ask for, because we want to win the war. But, Mr. President, the responsibility, which they agree to assume is one for which they will have to answer after the veil of secrecy has been lifted. I, for one, am now giving notice that when the veil of secrecy shall have been lifted I shall want to know, in behalf of the people of this country, and in a detailed way, why those to whom I have referred assumed such responsibility at such a critical time.[34]

In 1946, the Committee asked Admiral Ernest J. King, for the Joint Chiefs, to furnish it with a statement as to the specific information on which its decision of October 26, 1943, had been based. The reply, the Committee said, "was in nowise informative, consisting of nothing beyond the reiterated opinion that the project was essential to military plans never yet disclosed." [35]

On September 3, 1946, the Committee presented its Fifth Annual Report to the Senate. The report, summing up the results of the project, said that the first crude was delivered to Whitehorse through the pipeline on April 16, 1944, but that no 100-octane gasoline was produced until October 31, 1944. The refinery operations were closed down on April 5, 1945. The total production of the project consisted of 23,417 barrels of aviation gasoline, 31,370 barrels of motor gasoline, and 256,358 barrels

of diesel oil. Assuming that diesel oil was desired in this propor-
tion to gasoline, one average-sized tanker could have delivered
the entire output of the project in approximately three months.
The tanker could have delivered more than that amount of gasoline in one 30-day trip.[36]

The report was critical of Somervell and Admiral King, but
did not make it entirely clear that King had acted for all four
of the Joint Chiefs. King charged the Committee with distortion
of the facts, and a public hearing was held. There was little difficulty in straightening out this difference, but the hearing served
a useful purpose in that the Committee succeeded in getting the
entire file of the Joint Chiefs on the Canol Project declassified
before the hearing. It insisted on this, since King was able to
review the files before his appearance.

King stated firmly that the Joint Chiefs in their decision of
October 26, 1943, had not gone into the case but had affirmed
the recommendations of the Joint Production Survey Committee.[37] The hearing also brought out the information that early in
1945 the Joint Production Survey Committee, the Army-Navy
Petroleum Board, and the Joint Chiefs concluded:

> Because of their limited capacity and the availability and necessity
> of other sources of supply, the Norman Wells to Whitehorse crude
> pipeline and the refinery at Whitehorse have no permanent defense
> value.[38]

The Canadian military authorities concurred in this view, and
the refinery was later sold to the Imperial Oil Company for
$1,000,000 and dismantled. The pipeline was auctioned off as
junk for $700,000. "This was the total reclaim value," one in-
vestigator observed.[39]

CONCLUSION

The Canol Project cost a total of approximately $134,000,000,
exclusive of the cost of Army personnel and Army air transpor-

tation, which were used extensively on the project (at one time there were 4,000 troops and 12,000 civilians engaged in it). Of the total, about $35,000,000 was spent on the militarily useful distribution pipelines. The balance was spent on the refinery, the Norman to Whitehorse pipeline, the development of transportation routes to get the materials there, and prospecting in the Norman area. This was virtually a total loss. The money itself was not very important in comparison with total war expenditures. But the funds represented the use of critical materials and manpower which were in short supply. It is clear that the materials used in the Canol Project could have been used to provide more petroleum elsewhere as well as the tankers to carry it to Alaska, at less cost in manpower. And at the time Patterson was asserting that the Canol Project was a military necessity he was protesting the production of even such essential items as automobile parts and railroad equipment.

Somervell doubtless believed sincerely that the project's petroleum production would be greater than it was. But he was warned repeatedly by persons who were better informed than he that the project would fail. Yet he paid no attention. The engineering challenge of the project probably appealed to his imagination, but this was no basis for a decision of such importance.

The Army's handling of the affair after the difficulties were called to its attention makes reasonable the interpretation that it refused to admit a mistake and was covering up. The decision of the Joint Chiefs served to put the project beyond the reach of civilian agencies and Congress by labeling it "strategic." John D. Millett, who had access to the files, reports that the Joint Production Survey Committee really had a strategic reason to continue the project: to keep the Japanese in a state of uncertainty as to the United States intentions with respect to an attack on Japan from the north.[40] The writer is extremely skeptical of this as a reason; it may have been a justification. If it was a reason, doubts are raised as to the abilities of the men on whom the Joint Chiefs were relying for staff work. For at this time the Army was withdrawing all possible troops from Alaska and deploying them to places where they would be of more value. In this process, military facilities were being reduced in scope and some were put in caretaker status. It is difficult to take seriously the contention that the abandonment of a petroleum project which was not producing petroleum would have informed the Japanese that the United States was not contemplating an attack from that direction while the virtual abandonment of military facilities would not. Furthermore, a strategic consideration such as that would presumably have been discussed by the Joint Chiefs themselves. But Admiral King, who also had access to the files, did not mention it while striving to justify the decision to the Committee.

This case illustrates the difficulty of civilian agencies in asserting their authority unless it is very clearly defined and established before a particular project comes under military control. Any strategic considerations were trivial; the Canol Project was an oil-production enterprise, and as such should have been under the control of the relevant civilian agency or should have had its approval. By labeling the project "strategic" the Army was able to protect itself against civilian influence.

The label also protected it against Congress. The Truman Committee's investigation of the Canol Project was one of its most thorough. It amply demonstrated the deficiencies of the project, but under its rules it did not attempt to interfere with strategic matters and left the matter to the military after the Joint Chiefs acted. Perhaps the Committee could have been more effective in enforcing its will on the military in this case. It might have questioned Patterson's and Somervell's personal motives instead of confining its criticisms to their judgments and actions, or it might have raised a public clamor against the project. But such courses would have risked impairing public confidence in the whole military establishment and would have violated the Committee's basic ideas on responsibility. They were never considered.

The case also demonstrated the realism of the assumption on which the Truman Committee was established: that it was better to investigate while the war was going on than to conduct post mortems. The review of the Canol Project after the war completed the record, but there was nothing else to be done.

6) The Committee and Big Business: The Curtiss-Wright Inspection Case

Patriotism is a very beautiful thing but it must not be permitted to interfere with business.[1]

THE ISSUE

In January, 1943, the Truman Committee instituted a preliminary investigation of complaints concerning the Wright Aeronautical Corporation at Lockland, Ohio. Wright Aeronautical Corporation was a wholly owned subsidiary of the Curtiss-Wright Corporation. The Lockland plant was the only facility producing several variations of a particular air-cooled engine of Wright's design. The plant had been built for that purpose at government expense, and it was considered an excellent plant for engine production. The plant and equipment were still owned by the United States government through the Defense Plant Corporation and the engines were being purchased under a fixed-price contract. Of eight engine plants Wright operated at that time, one was its own, one had been built by the British, and six had been built by the United States government.

The complaints were serious. They were made by a number of inspectors at the Lockland plant, who alleged that improper inspection at the plant was resulting in delivery of defective engines and parts to the Air Force. One inspector broke down and cried as he told the Committee investigator his story, saying that he had two nephews in the Air Force.[2]

The preliminary investigation indicated that there was a substantial basis for the complaints and that if they were true they should have been known to top company and Army officials. At the request of both the company and the Army, the Committee withheld further investigation to allow them to make their own investigations and report back to the Committee "any improper conditions they found and any corrective measures which were being taken." [3]

After allowing over a week for these investigations, the Committee held a private hearing in Washington on March 30, 1943. Brigadier General Bennett E. Meyers, testifying for the Army, told the Committee that his office had found nothing wrong with inspection or management at the plant. C. G. Poehlmann, quality manager of the plant, and W. H. Finlay, manager, said they knew of a few "incidents and errors that have been corrected," and characterized them thus: "The talk and incidents weren't of a character in relation to inspection. There was more petty bickering over privileges, authority, and rights." [4]

Beginning two days later, a subcommittee of the Committee held closed hearings in Washington, Cincinnati, and Dayton, Ohio, taking a total of 1,286 pages of sworn testimony. It found a situation greatly at variance with that presented to it by the Air Force and the company. It found that the company *was* delivering defective products to the government, and that this was accomplished:

1. By the falsification of tests.
2. By destruction of records.
3. By improperly recording results of tests.
4. By forging inspection reports.

5. By failing to segregate substandard and defective material.
6. By failing to promptly destroy or mutilate such defective and substandard material.
7. By orally changing tolerances allowed on parts.
8. By circumventing the salvage committee set up to pass on the usability of parts outside tolerances.
9. By allowing production to override the inspection force, thereby destroying the morale of both company and Army inspectors.
10. By skipping inspection operations.[5]

The primary responsibility for inspection was the company's. It had been awarded an A inspection rating by the Army Air Force, which meant that the Army kept only a small force of inspectors (seventy, as against 2,400 for the company) at the plant for spot checking. The Committee felt that the inspection system was adequate "if, and only if, both company and Air Force personnel are sincere and honest in their effort to produce a quality product." [6]

Unfortunately, the Committee found that Army inspectors were more zealous in protecting the welfare of the company than in protecting the interests of the Air Force. "It was found," its report said later, "that the feeling was deliberately fostered among Air Force inspectors that they must be cooperative with the company if they were to get along well in their jobs." [7] Inspectors were transferred for failing to get along with company personnel—a euphemism for refusing to accept defective material for the government. They were threatened with transfer or other disciplinary action for not accepting engines with even serious defects. The Committee found that even while its investigation was being conducted one inspector was transferred solely because he refused to accept an engine which was leaking gasoline. Inspectors were discouraged from doing an effective job by the company practice of taking rejections through an extended appeals procedure in which the inspector was almost invariably overruled at some point. Army inspectors were also refused access to precision instruments (which the company was supposed to furnish) for checking material and were denied the use of rejection stamps, making it impossible to check on the later use of rejected parts.

It was maintained before the Committee that, in spite of irregularities, no harm had been done, but the Committee definitely established that:

1. Engines that leaked gasoline had been sold to the government, although no engine with a gas leak of any kind was acceptable or safe.

2. Unsafe material had been found in engines ready for shipment.

3. A substantial number of planes using this engine had crashed because of engine failures. There was, of course, no way to attribute these to faulty inspection, but the Air Force undertook a check of all engines produced during the period of the Committee's investigation.

4. Consistently, more than 25 per cent of the engines produced at the Lockland plant had failed in one or more major parts during 3-hour test runs.

5. Spare parts had been delivered without inspection.

6. The records of the Army showed that from 1941, when the plant began producing engines, until the investigation, it had been impossible to complete successfully a required 150-hour quality test.[8]

That some Army Air Forces officers were abetting the company in these practices was indicated by their behavior and testimony. Led by the Chief Inspector at Lockland for the Army Air Forces, these officials, the Committee reported, "made misstatements under oath," attempted to intimidate witnesses, and prepared false evidence designed to discredit witnesses testifying as to the conditions at the plant.[9] The Committee was given personnel files of four inspectors who had insisted on rejecting substandard material and who had been removed. The file indicated that the four had been "troublemakers," but the Committee discovered that the file had been prepared a day or two before the hearing and was not the file of their employment.[10]

The record of the testimony taken at these closed hearings was turned over to the Army, and at the request of the Army Air Force no further action was taken by the Committee pending investigation and corrective action.

This investigation was conducted in two parts. The Air Inspector, after some delay, undertook an investigation of the misconduct of Air Force officers, which resulted eventually in the trial of the culpable officers. The Assistant Secretary of War for Air, Robert A. Lovett, also convened an investigatory board, headed by Lieutenant General William S. Knudsen (when the WPB was established he was commissioned and put in charge of production). Miles H. Knowles, who was handling Congressional investigations for the Army, had gone to Cincinnati with the subcommittee. He had been permitted to cross-examine witnesses, go through the plant, and make his own investigation. Upon his return to Washington he prepared a report for Lovett which listed eighteen findings of conditions that were wrong at the Lockland plant. Knowles recommended that Lovett accompany him to Cincinnati to see about correcting the conditions there. Instead, Lovett appointed the board.[11]

The Board began its investigation promptly. It issued a preliminary report on April 17 and a final report on June 28, 1943. It promptly removed the A inspection rating from the plant. There were some personnel changes in the inspection force at Lockland, and Major General Charles E. Branshaw was put in charge of the Air Forces Materiel Command, a change heartily approved by the Committee.

The Knudsen Board report, which was written by William O'Dwyer, apparently treated Knowles's report to Lovett as a

Committee report. Without Knowles's knowledge, the board's report was cleared and sent to the Committee. Knowles said later that his findings had been belittled and answered with "weasel words." [12] The Board actually made the same findings of fact as the Committee and Knowles but treated the situation rather lightly and avoided attributing culpability to anyone. It reported that "careless inspection existed throughout the plant" and that unsafe material had been found in engines ready for shipment; but the Board ignored, according to the Committee, the open and deliberate faking of certain tests.[13] The Board did find and indicated that it viewed the condition as unhealthy, that:

. . . there is prevalent among both Government and company inspectors the feeling that considerably less difficulty will be encountered if they pass a questionable part than will be encountered if they reject a questionable part. It is reasonable to believe that the easier course was frequently followed.[14]

The Board agreed that one of the reasons for this was that government inspectors were frequently overruled by superiors and threatened with transfer if there were too many rejections.

The Board stated that the use of rejection stamps had been abolished at the request of the company even before the Lockland plant had been built. This was done because the parts, even though rejected by the government, "could be and were sold to commercial accounts and to foreign governments." This would have been more difficult if the parts were stamped as rejected by the government. The Knudsen Board not only saw nothing wrong in this practice, but deplored the feeling that the elimination of the rejection stamps was an effort to pass inferior material.[15]

These facts were made public on July 10, 1943, as part of a comprehensive Committee report on aircraft. The report contained a discussion of the Knudsen Board's report, on which it concluded: "In general it may be stated that the Board's report is accurate in the matter of stating facts but assumes an unnecessarily defensive attitude." [16] The Committee noted that some changes had been made to tighten up Army and company inspection, and it indicated that the Air Forces were undertaking to trace and check every engine produced in the plant during the period when it was believed the unsatisfactory conditions existed. The Committee thought this check should reduce the chances that defective engines would get into service, but did not suggest that Curtiss-Wright bear the cost of this expensive and time-consuming check. It recommended, however, that the War Department renegotiate its contracts with Curtiss-Wright on the grounds that the fees paid the company were for management which had been represented "to be the finest in the world" but which had proved inadequate.[17]

The Committee, in trying to assess the reasons for the state of affairs at Curtiss-Wright, returned to its theme of the concentration of contracts, stating:

> The Committee is of the opinion that the Lockland plant is a glaring example of the concentration of contracts in large plants with inexperienced management trying to get out a large production on a fixed-price contract and ruthlessly slashing quality to maintain production and schedules in the face of excessive production costs caused by poor management.[18]

The Committee blamed the Army and Navy for a tendency to multiply the capacity of plants and companies with which contracts were already established rather than seeking additional sources of supply. It criticized the Army in this case for bypassing inspection to protect the reputation of the company.

The report noted that this case raised a question about the contention of the Armed Forces that "they and they alone were capable of procuring safe and satisfactory material for the fighting forces and that for that reason no civilian agency should ever have anything to say with reference to such matters." [19]

The report did not note that the case also raised a question with respect to the widely held assumption, which the Committee shared, that fixed-price contracts were necessarily the means to efficient production.

As the Committee followed its usual procedure of submitting reports before publication to all interested parties, Curtiss-Wright was not unprepared when the report was made public. The same day, Guy Warner Vaughan, president of both the Curtiss-Wright and Wright Aeronautical Corporations, stated to the press:

The company emphatically denies the statement made by the Committee that the Wright Aeronautical Corporation has at any time sold or delivered to the Government, or anyone else, products known to the company to have contained defective or substandard parts. Wright has categorically denied this specific allegation and insists on its right now and at all times to repudiate as false and unwarranted any such charges.[20]

Vaughan said flatly that the inevitable mistakes accompanying an expansion as great as that undertaken by Curtiss-Wright had "in no way affected the finished products which have been flowing in such vast quantities from our production lines to our fighting forces on various battle fronts." He asserted that the company had not undertaken its expansion of its own volition, but "as a patriotic duty." [21]

Curtiss-Wright also launched an advertising campaign featuring both Vaughan's statement and claims that Curtiss engines were making a magnificent contribution toward winning the war. Some of the advertisements stated that engines made at Lockland powered the B-25 bombers that participated in the Tokyo raid. Simultaneously there appeared a number of newspaper stories implying that the investigation had hurt production, which at Lockland dropped 85 per cent between March and July. And there was a tendency in the press to play down the charges in favor of the production record of Curtiss-Wright.[22]

The response to its report induced the Committee to conduct public hearings to put the facts on the record. These began on August 20, 1943, in Cincinnati.

The first witness was Major General Oliver P. Echols, Assistant Chief, Air Staff in Charge of Materiel, Maintenance, and Distribution, Army Air Forces. General Echols testified to the changes made in the personnel responsible for Army inspection in order to ensure that proper inspection would be carried out. He emphasized that such inspection was not picayunish but was based on tolerances and standards established by the company when it designed the engine, and he added that the company had never complained to the Air Forces that these were too strict. Although he had received reports from the company that many of the production difficulties were due to changes in the inspection procedures, he stressed emphatically that the procedures were only those that should have been followed at all times to ensure an acceptable product.[23] Senator Kilgore, in an unannounced visit to the plant a few days before the hearings began, had discovered evidence that 700 engines, packed in grease and boxed ready for shipment, were stored in a warehouse.[24] He was convinced that the company was trying to make a case for the Army's and the Committee's interfering with production. He asked General Echols about this, and the General agreed that the drop in production was certainly caused in part by "the fact that the management in the plant persisted in trying to blame the Army for interference with production." [25] When Echols stated that Army inspection delays could not account for a drop of more than a few engines a month, Hugh Fulton pointed out that only two interpretations of the drastic drop in production were possible: "Either they never were able to produce [the normal output of] good engines, or they have deliberately refrained from producing them, or a combination of the two." [26]

Major Frank W. LaVista, the Army's new chief of inspection at Lockland, was even more definite. He had reported to the Army, and repeated to the Committee, that he had asked company officials for specific instances of delay due to Army inspections and that they had been unable to name one. His explanation of the low production in July (his first month on duty) was that over 400 engines had been rejected because of high oil flow caused by "the fact that no effort was made to maintain a close tolerance on the connecting rod bearings." [27] Thirty-three of these engines were reassembled with a "select fit" on the bearings, and all were able to pass. This meant that parts near the upper limit of tolerance acceptability, for instance, were fitted with other parts near the upper limit. Use of this procedure on all engines would have eliminated the source of most of the connecting rod difficulties.

Major LaVista told the Committee that three days after the appearance of the ads denying any shipment of defective materials he took three engines that were finally inspected and sealed, ready for shipping, brought them back, took them apart, and completely reinspected them. "Every one of the three engines," he said, "were found to be in such condition that they could not have been installed in an airplane." [28] They were so bad that the company recalled eighty-nine engines ready for shipment and reinspected them the same way. Most were found to be defective, although not as seriously as the first three, which had missing lockwires, corroded parts, and dry cylinders.

The major also testified that only one case of other-than-routine inspection had been referred to the Army during July and that it had been decided within an hour. He said he had taken action on several occasions to prevent the company's be-

coming hypertechnical, the latest time being the day after Kilgore's surprise visit to the plant (with a subcommittee).[29]

Major LaVista was followed by Vaughan. He disclaimed responsibility for and repudiated the stories attributing the drop
in production to the Truman Committee and absolved the Army
of any responsibility. But he maintained that the publicity connected with the investigation was hurting morale and contributing to the delay in resumption of full production. Vaughan was
sharply questioned about his statement that no defective material
was delivered:

> *Mr. Fulton.* In the light of that testimony [LaVista's], Mr.
> Vaughan, do you still take the position that your inspection proce-
> dures are such that no matter how lax you may be in any given part
> of the work, a finished engine which is defective cannot get through
> and does not get through?
> *Mr. Vaughan.* Well, I say there is no record of any engine that
> we know of—
> *Mr. Fulton (interposing).* But you now have three.
> *Mr. Vaughan.* I don't know whether you are thoroughly fa-
> miliar with motors, but I wouldn't call it a defective engine in that
> sense.
> *Mr. Fulton.* Would you put those three motors, with defects of
> the character described by Major LaVista, into an airplane?
> *Mr. Vaughan.* No, sir; not if I found them.
> *Mr. Fulton.* And you hadn't found them, had you?
> *Mr. Vaughan.* Apparently not, from the records.
>
> *   *   *   *   *   *
>
> *Mr. Fulton.* What I am saying is that here are cases, three en-
> gines specifically, eighty-nine others which Major LaVista has not
> described so specifically, but has characterized as having defects. Do
> you still take the position on behalf of Curtiss-Wright and Wright
> Aeronautical Corporation that defective engines or engines with de-
> fective parts did not get out into service?
> *Mr. Vaughan.* I say that we never knew or never had anything
> that we knew was defective get out of the plant, and we never have
> shipped what I would call a defective engine. An engine is made up

of several thousand parts, and if there is a little corrosion on one piece, it is highly technical to call it a defect.

> *Mr. Fulton.* What do you call it?
>
> *Mr. Vaughan.* I call it an oversight that has got to be fixed. . . .[30]

Vaughan admitted that these engines would have been shipped except for the Committee's investigation, which led the questioning into the matter that was exciting much of the Committee's ire—the advertisements. The Committee hammered at the phrase "known to the company" in Vaughan's statement to the press. Vaughan defined the company as himself and the responsible officers, including plant managers. He admitted that he had not known whether the manager at Lockland knew about defective material when he had made the statement. He said that he did not know whether Lockland-made engines had been used in the Tokyo raid, and later wrote a letter to Truman stating that investigation had shown that they had not.[31] He insisted, however, that the advertisements told the truth. He stated that they were inserted in papers in the area of their plants near Cincinnati, Ohio and Paterson, New Jersey, "only for the purpose of bringing up the morale of the men," to which Fulton replied, "Wasn't the best way to put somebody in there competent to manage the plant and make it operate?" [32]

When asked about the ads in papers in New York City, Washington, and Detroit and in national magazines such as *Collier's,* Vaughan replied that they were for the stockholders. He steadfastly denied that the purpose of the ads was to influence public opinion, but he did not convince the Committee.

One of the things about the advertising campaign that disturbed the Committee was that virtually all of the cost of the campaign was borne by the government, since Curtiss-Wright was being taxed at the maximum excess-profits tax rate and its contracts were subject to renegotiation. The Committee uncovered the information that the ads in the Cincinnati and Paterson

areas alone had cost a total of almost $6,000 [33] and that the
company expected to spend in 1943 more than $870,000 on
institutional advertising—that is, advertising designed to bolster
the company's public image rather than sell goods to consumers.
The campaign included ads praising the Curtiss-Wright Hell-
diver as the "world's best dive bomber" when it had not produced a single one that the Navy considered usable as a combat
aircraft.[34] Fulton questioned Vaughan about this:

> *Mr. Fulton.* . . . your company is subject to renegotiation on
> profits. If you reduce your profits by increasing your expenses
> through extra advertising, you thereby, in effect, charge the Govern-
> ment 100 per cent for your advertising.
> *Mr. Vaughan.*   If you did it with that in mind; yes.
> *Mr. Fulton.*   Whatever way you do it, whatever your purpose,
> that is the effect.
> *Mr. Vaughan.*   We are doing it, believe it or not, in the conscien-
> tious effort to do the best job we know how from every point of view,
> and not just one or two points of view.
> *Mr. Fulton.*   Will you show us the ads that are in accordance—
> *Mr. Vaughan (interposing).*   Certainly.
> *Mr. Fulton.*   No: that are in accordance with your testimony to-
> day, that your company did have lax inspection procedures which
> this Committee and the Army, through their investigation, succeeded
> in changing? Where have you advertised that for the purpose of
> helping your morale?
> *Mr. Vaughan.*   Do you think it would help?
> *Mr. Fulton.*   I do, because it would show that you now were not
> doing what caused several scores of your people to write to the Tru-
> man Committee.[35]

In the end, under persistent cross-examination, Vaughan admitted the correctness of all the facts in the Committee's case,
although he continued to deny the culpability of anyone.

In its Third Annual Report, presented on March 3, 1944, the
Committee was able to report that it had received from Vaughan
a long letter detailing a major reorganization of the company's

engine division which he hoped would meet the Committee's criticisms and improve the efficiency of the corporation's operations. The Committee commended Major LaVista and General Branshaw for their efforts in cleaning up the situation at Lockland. General Branshaw, incidentally, had informed the Committee that the situation was three times worse than the Committee had said it was.[36]

One might expect that this experience would have made Vaughan rather sensitive to any suggestion that inspection in his company was not all it should be. But Vaughan was made of sterner stuff. On November 6, 1943, General Branshaw wrote to Vaughan concerning unsatisfactory conditions at the two Curtiss-Wright airplane plants at Buffalo, New York. Both of these plants were making the C-46, a Wright-designed transport and cargo plane. The unsatisfactory conditions had to do with inspection, failure to work out the "bugs" in an otherwise satisfactory plane, and inefficient utilization of manpower in the plant. Branshaw warned Vaughan that if quality control conditions were not cleared up there might be a repetition of the experience with investigation committees. On August 7, 1944, Branshaw's successor wrote again to Vaughan, registering much the same complaints about inspection at the plants.[37] During the intervening period various Air Force inspection personnel also called the matter to the company's attention.

In April, 1945, Senator William Langer criticized the inspection methods being used at the Buffalo plants of Curtiss-Wright on the floor of the Senate and requested the Mead Committee (Senator James M. Mead had succeeded Truman as chairman) to investigate. The company also requested the investigation. Consequently, the Committee held closed hearings in Washington in June, and four days of public hearings in Buffalo in July. The report, issued July 26, found that inspection procedures were inadequate, caused by chaotic conditions resulting from efforts to step up production schedules substantially. The Committee was unable to determine if the planes were defective, but noted in its report that "production was dominating inspection throughout the plant and it must be reasonably assumed that this did affect the quality of the end product airplane." [38]

It reported that conditions had improved somewhat since the fall of 1944, but blamed both the Army and the company for continued laxness in inspection.

The report was sharply critical of Curtiss-Wright for a lack of interest in correcting shortcomings. Vaughan could not remember ever having received the letters mentioned above! [39] And the Committee had found at least two cases where company inspectors had been dismissed "for insisting that plane parts be installed according to specifications." [40] When the Committee discussed these conditions with company officials, "they attempted to excuse or minimize the situation and generally exhibited a lack of vigor in promptly locating and correcting the unsatisfactory conditions, of which they were cognizant." [41]

The Committee made no findings as to culpability and, with the ending of the war shortly after this report was issued, turned its attention to matters connected with reconversion. The question of the integrity of inspection at Curtiss-Wright was obviated by the cancellation of most of its contracts following the end of the war.

CONCLUSION

Curtiss-Wright received a total of over $7 billion worth of war contracts, second in dollar volume only to General Motors. To enable it to produce this volume of goods, its facilities were greatly expanded at government expense. Undoubtedly this resulted in the company's experienced management being "spread too thin," which could explain careless inspection by inexperienced personnel trying to achieve a high level of production. It does not explain the disciplining of inspectors who did a conscientious job, nor the reluctance to correct the situation when it was pointed out, nor the obstruction of the Truman Committee's efforts to uncover the facts in order that they might be corrected. These things suggest that Curtiss-Wright was more interested in its own welfare than in its duty in the struggle in which its products were playing an important part.

A great responsibility was placed on the companies that received enormous contracts for war material. Much of the responsibility for the quality of the product was upon them, with the procurement agencies performing only spot checks. The controls to ensure the orderly production of the items as they were needed also required a high degree of voluntary compliance. Only a few companies deliberately shipped the government unsatisfactory goods, although included among them were several of the leaders of American industry. But many more were guilty of lesser crimes—refusal to convert to war production, violation of priorities and allocations regulations, evasion of taxes, and ignoring or violation of other controls. Edwin H. Sutherland, in studying the behavior of seventy large corporations, found that virtually all of them were guilty of at least one "war crime." He concluded, "This evidence raises a question whether these corporations are not driven by self-interest to such an extent that they are constitutionally unable to participate in the cooperative life of society." [42]

The Truman Committee never evinced any recognition that there might be such a problem. Throughout the war the Committee rather took it for granted that the free operation of the profit motive would produce efficient production. It is probable that the fixed-price contract was more effective than the cost-plus-a-fixed-fee contract in protecting the interests of the government. But it did not do so automatically, and the Committee had ample evidence to this effect. The Committee treated as isolated

examples the cases in which obligations to the government had
been ignored in the quest for profit, and appears not to have
looked for implications that might have been raised by them.

In part this was due to the fact that the Committee members
accepted the dominant values of American society. In part it
may have been due to the responses it encountered in its conflicts with big industry. In cases of corruption involving some
of the many individuals who used the war as an opportunity to
get rich quick, the Committee usually found the press on its side.
But in the Carnegie-Illinois and Curtiss-Wright cases, both of
which involved fraudulent inspection by leading corporations,
the Committee's revelations were greeted with a spate of articles
in periodicals to the effect that the Committee was hurting production or that its findings were bad for morale and should
have been kept quiet. It had some press support in these cases,
of course, but there was decidedly not unanimity.

In addition, in the Curtiss-Wright case the Committee had to
face an advertising campaign challenging its findings. The Committee objected strongly to this advertising in that it was misleading or untrue, and it raised the issue of whether the government
ought to accept, as a cost of doing business, excessive institutional advertising especially when it was devoted to exaggerated
self-praise. The Committee did not, however, raise the question
of whether the government should have to bear the burden of the
cost of institutional advertising when that advertising bore no
relation to the job being done for the government.

The reaction of the advertising industry to even this mild
criticism of institutional advertising was prompt and sharp, for
advertising men and publishers were fearful throughout the war
that Congress might restrict or prohibit the deduction, as an
expense of doing business for tax purposes, of the vast sums of
money spent on institutional advertising. Shortly after the Truman Committee criticized Curtiss-Wright's use of misleading

advertising, James H. McGraw, Jr., President of McGraw-Hill, contacted Hugh Fulton to arrange a meeting between Fulton and the Committee members and a number of people interested in advertising, including McGraw and Roy E. Larsen of Time, Inc., so that they could explain to the Committee the importance of advertising. Willard Chalier, Publisher of *Business Week,* prepared a memorandum on advertising for the Committee. Some of the ideas contained in this memo were apparently incorporated by Fulton in a speech given by Truman to the American Association of Advertising Agencies, and Paul B. West, who was in the office of the President of the Association of National Advertisers, also contributed to it. In the speech, Truman assured the industry that the Committee was not criticizing institutional advertising as such but only the use of advertising to cover up deficiencies or shortcomings and its use by companies that had no brand names to keep before the public. He suggested that the advertising industry should itself police abuses, but his suggestion bore little fruit.[43]

On the other hand, the Committee did succeed in exerting sufficient pressure to get the Curtiss-Wright situation straightened out, and it was not the fault of the Committee that it recurred. A Congressional committee is not well equipped to deal with broad social issues, but it can be effective in bringing specific problems to public attention, as the Truman Committee repeatedly demonstrated.

The Army Air Forces had expanded more rapidly than the other services and had little experience with the problems of procurement. The behavior of some of its officers in this case resulted partly from its experienced personnel being spread too thin. Another factor was the Army's reluctance to admit mistakes, which Knowles found to be rather characteristic (though he found the Air Force worse than the Army in this respect). It is clear that some of the officers saw the company and themselves in alliance against a common Congressional enemy rather than the Committee as an ally in doing a job. Here, also, the Committee was able to exert sufficient pressure to bring personnel changes and improvement of procedures, with salutary effect in the Air Force procurement program.

Again it should be noted that the Committee behaved responsibly. Although it was dealing with an issue which it could exploit to arouse public opinion, it gave the Army and the company ample opportunity to correct the wrongs before putting its information before the public. When its findings were attacked, the Committee then demonstrated to the public that it was right. Even then, and later when it was criticized in ads and editorials, the Truman Committee sought primarily to shoot at conditions to be corrected rather than to pillory individuals.

7)   Conclusions

*There is some scandal and discomfort, but infinite advantage, in hav-
ing every affair of administration subjected to the test of constant
examination on the part of the assembly which represents the nation.
The chief use of such inquisition is, not the direction of those affairs
in a way with which the country will be satisfied (though that itself
is of course all-important), but the enlightenment of the people,
which is always its sure consequence. Very few men are unequal to a
danger which they see and understand; all men quail before a threat-
ening which is dark and unintelligible, and suspect what is done behind a screen. If the people could have, through Congress, daily
knowledge of all the more important transactions of the governmental offices, an insight into all that now seems withheld and private, their confidence in the executive, now so often shaken, would, I
think be very soon established.*

Woodrow Wilson [1]

GENERAL SUMMARY

The Senate Special Committee to Investigate the National Defense Program existed for seven years, from 1941 to 1948, covering most of the defense period and the war years and extend-
ing beyond the point where most Americans lost all interest in
the war program. The resolution that created it gave the Committee almost unlimited authority to review the war effort, which

it used to cover almost all aspects of the war program except strategy and tactics.

The Committee was not hampered by lack of funds. After it gained prominence, the Committee had little difficulty getting funds for its activities from the Senate. In all, it received a total of $925,000 which was spent for staff salaries, office supplies, traveling expenses, and the reporting of its hearings.

During its tenure the Committee issued fifty-one reports, including two minority reports (both issued in 1948) totaling 1,946 pages. It held 432 public hearings at which 1,798 witnesses made 2,284 appearances, producing forty-three volumes of printed testimony totaling 27,568 pages. It held approximately 300 private hearings, taking 25,000 additional pages of transcript. Many of these private hearings covered subjects also covered in public hearings, and some testimony taken in private hearings was later released to become a part of the public record. The Committee also handled several hundred cases by correspondence and conferences in which no hearings were held. To complete the statistical survey, it may be recorded that the Committee turned over to the National Archives some ninety-four filing cases of records, which the Archives now lists at 580 feet.[2] The Committee records constitute an almost inexhaustible fund of information about the war economy of the United States.

The work of the Committee may be divided into several broad categories, in which there is inevitably some overlap: (1) the recurrent examination of continuing problems of war mobilization and the efforts to solve them; (2) investigation of shortages of critical materials and of specific programs to remedy them; (3) investigations of programs pertaining to the supply of equipment and facilities, including waste, inefficiency, and plain blunders associated with the program; (4) the investigation of war frauds, including fraudulent activities of war contractors, "influence peddlers," and government officials.

The examples of the work of the Committee in the preceding chapters represent each of the broad categories and serve to illustrate relations with various agencies. Each of the cases was important in itself; taken together they give a fairly balanced view of the types of Committee activities.

1. Probably the Committee's most constructive work was its studies of continuing problems of mobilization together with the arbitration of conflicts. As measured by the rough standard of volume of hearings, some 40 per cent of its work falls in this category. The Committee made real contributions to the war effort in its criticisms of the organization of the production agencies, which led to the establishment of the War Production Board, and in the very important support it lent Donald M. Nelson in carrying out his almost impossible duties. This interest in the organization of procurement continued, with efforts directed at securing centralized control over the production of both military and civilian goods. The continuing concern of the Committee with contract distribution was a factor in getting somewhat wider distribution of contracts and greater use of existing facilities than might otherwise have been the case. Its early examination of problems of renegotiation and reconversion helped to make public issues of these matters before it became too late to do anything about them. All phases of transportation received its scrutiny, as did the problems of labor and manpower, shipbuilding, use of shipping, and the disposal of surpluses.

Not all its suggestions were accepted, of course—not all were equally deserving of acceptance. And most of these problems received attention from other Congressional committees, sometimes with conflicting conclusions. The Truman Committee, for example, was very critical of the use of dollar-a-year men by the Office of Production Management and the War Production Board in its First Annual Report, and was likewise critical of the Aluminum Company of America in its report on aluminum. The House Military Affairs Committee, in an extensive report on the war effort issued in 1942, commended both.[3] In this same report the House Committee was much more critical of the War Department than the Truman Committee had been.

The Committee also investigated and served as arbiter in a number of conflicts and disputes between war agencies. Much of this work was done without publicity through private meetings between the disputants and the Committee members or counsel. The Committee was particularly active in the running battle that took place between the military and the WPB during most of the war period, and usually lined up with the WPB and civilian officials.

The Committee was especially critical of the military for having failed to plan adequately before the emergency for even such basic needs as camps and cantonments and for failure to plan carefully and accurately for its future needs so that these needs might be met on time. It was critical of the military for failing to coordinate the various and sometimes conflicting procurement programs and for concentrating contracts in a relatively few large producers. Such policies were detrimental to small business and wasteful of productive capacity.

The Committee prodded the Army on manpower planning, on its intelligence agencies, and on its recreational program. It prodded the Navy to experiment with helicopters and to produce landing craft. It chided the Air Force for permitting and even aiding fraudulent inspection and was severely critical of its investigative procedures. In short, it clashed with the military over a wide range of home-front matters throughout the war.

2. During the mobilization period a series of shortages of critical items plagued the procurement and production agencies. All of these were investigated by the Truman Committee as well as other Congressional committees, administrative agencies, and

special Presidential committees or boards. About 30 per cent of the Truman Committee's hearings were devoted to these investigations. The Committee's first report dealt with the shortage of aluminum and presented findings critical of OPM for relying upon the Aluminum Company of America, a company which was primarily interested in avoiding "the possibility that anyone else would go into a field which they had for so many years successfully monopolized." [4] Investigations of shipbuilding, nonferrous and light metals, fuel oil and gasoline, housing, lumber, petroleum, mica, steel, and rubber followed as the shortages appeared.

One of the most critical shortages the United States faced during the war was of rubber. On May 26, 1943, the Committee issued a report that examined the rubber shortage and the steps taken to remedy it. The report faced the possibility of the necessity for nationwide gasoline rationing as a measure for conserving rubber but did not recommend it, although the Committee did so later. The report discussed at some length the cartel arrangements between Standard Oil Company of New Jersey and I. G. Farben, which had been a factor in delaying the development of synthetic rubber in this country. It noted that no question of moral turpitude or "subjective unpatriotic motive" was involved, but that it was "part of a general picture of big business playing the game according to the rules," although a heavy price had "to be borne by the entire Nation." [5]

The report was extremely critical of the diffusion of responsibility for the rubber program and recommended "that some one person should exercise full responsibility, and accordingly, full power to take all necessary action to provide such rubber as is necessary to the war program, subject only to responsibility to Mr. Nelson." [6] It took no position on the controversial question of whether to emphasize the production of butadiene from petroleum or from grain alcohol, merely recommending consideration of all possible methods.

The rubber shortage was probably the most studied supply problem of the war; ten or twelve committees investigated it at some time. A subcommittee of the Senate Agriculture Committee under Senator Guy M. Gillette vigorously supported a bill to set up an independent rubber supply agency and to push the use of grain alcohol for making butadiene. This bill (S.2600) was passed by Congress in July, 1942, although opposed by the Administration and Senators from oil-producing states. In spite of the Truman Committee's interest in the matter and its recognition of the danger of diluting the power of the WPB by setting up independent agencies concerned with specific programs, no member of the Committee took part in the debate on S.2600.

President Roosevelt promptly vetoed the bill because of its establishment of an independent agency, but he sought to mollify Congress by appointing a committee consisting of Bernard M. Baruch, Dr. James B. Conant, and Karl T. Compton to investigate the problem and report to him. The result was the appointment, in September, 1942, of a Rubber Director under Nelson with full authority over the rubber program. The Truman Committee later took credit for these developments, but it is difficult to avoid the conclusion that if it had pushed its own recommendations more forcefully and opposed S.2600 vigorously the result might have been achieved several months earlier. On the other hand, the Committee played an important role in strengthening Nelson in the later conflict between the rubber program and the programs for 100-octane gasoline and escort vessels.

3. The Committee's second report dealt with the problem which had inspired Truman's resolution—the camp and cantonment construction program. The Committee reported incredible waste and inefficiency. A comparison of costs showed that the average cost per man of seventeen camps constructed on a

lump-sum basis was $380, while the cost per man of twenty-nine camps constructed on a cost-plus-fixed-fee basis was $684.[7] The Committee recommended that all construction be transferred from the jurisdiction of the Quartermaster Corps to the Corps of Engineers and called for a number of improvements in the handling of contracts. These recommendations were adopted, effecting a monetary saving estimated by Lieutenant General Brehon B. Somervell to be $250 million.[8]

Shipbuilding, landing craft, the Canol Project, the inter-American highway, ordnance plants, manufacturing facilities, and defense housing were included in the Committee's scrutiny of the procurement of facilities and equipment. Some of these investigations involved prodding the responsible agencies into action, some sought to remove sources of waste and inefficiency, and some were aimed at correcting blunders, as in the case of the Canol Project. A few of these investigations uncovered evidence of near corruption and fraud. For example, in its investigation of the Wolf Creek Ordnance Plant, the Committee found excessive fees, nepotism, poor construction, payroll loading, and extortion. The Committee was especially critical of the War Department for failing to conduct an adequate investigation of these matters after they had been called to its attention.[9] In all, about 10 per cent of the Committee's hearings were devoted to subjects within this category.

4. The tremendous sums of money being spent for war goods offered unparalleled opportunities for a quick fortune to the enterprising and unscrupulous. Small businessmen whose previous business was limited to thousands of dollars saw them reach the millions, and many saw the opportunity to parlay little or no capital into a fortune with the help of war contracts and some influence. The Committee investigated a number of such cases, including the Wolf Creek Ordnance Plant, the Empire Ordnance Corporation, a number of construction firms, and the

May-Garsson operations. About 20 per cent of its hearings were devoted to frauds. Some nefarious practices were voluntarily halted as a result of these investigations, and a few persons were indicted, convicted and sent to jail for their activities. The Committee was less forthright and less successful in getting something done to prevent such practices in the future. Although it conducted hearings on lobbying and influence peddling in December, 1941, and reported on them to the Senate in its First Annual Report, its comments were not very vigorous. It recognized that small-business men sought to obtain the influence big business obtained with its dollar-a-year men by hiring people they thought had influence. The Committee condemned the practice and some of those who had engaged in it, but recognized that some lobbyists performed legitimate services. However, it held that the fees received obviously were based on expectations of services that went far beyond those rendered. The Committee recommended tightening the laws with respect to the practice of governmental employees who left the government for private employment and then sought business from the government, and said it planned to hold further hearings on the subject. The hearings were never held, although the subject came up in hearings held on other matters such as renegotiation and in some of the hearings dealing with specific frauds. The laws were relaxed by Congress rather than tightened,[10] but the Committee cannot be blamed for that.

War frauds were not committed only by promoters trying to make a stake in a hurry. Unfortunately, some of the largest corporations in the United States, including several which had the largest war contracts, were guilty of outright fraud upon the government. The Committee investigated a number of such cases—one was the case of fraudulent inspection practices on the part of the Carnegie-Illinois Steel Company, a subsidiary of the United States Steel Corporation. Although the Committee condemned these frauds in vigorous terms, it was somewhat reluctant to place the blame and responsibility at the highest levels within these corporations. Even though the management of Carnegie-Illinois denied any knowledge of the fraudulent inspection, it put every obstacle in the way of the Committee's investigation. After it was forced to admit the practices and to promise a clean-up, Senator Brewster asked a key question for which the president of U. S. Steel had no answer: "You realize, Mr. Fairless, how incredible it seems that subordinates in the company would risk their entire future without hope of reward of any character. That, of course, is what impresses the committee and makes it so amazing." [11] In its report on this case, however, the Committee was content to insist on honest inspection and accepted the assurances of the company that it would be achieved.

Several other cases investigated by the Committee involved highly placed individuals, including Representative Andrew J. May, Chairman of the House Military Affairs Committee; Senator Theodore G. Bilbo; Brigadier General Bennett E. Meyers of the Air Force; "Happy" Chandler and his swimming pool. As an aftermath of the Committee's investigations Representative May and General Meyers were convicted and received prison sentences. In these cases, the Department of Justice took over from the Committee and gathered the evidence of individual wrongdoing.

In all, the Truman Committee conducted four investigations involving members of Congress, three mentioned above and one concerning Representative John M. Coffee. The investigation of Representative Coffee consisted of a hearing in 1946 to determine whether a $2,500 check from a contractor was a genuine campaign contribution or was payment for services rendered in getting contracts. No report was issued.[12] There were partisan overtones to the case and it was an issue on which most Congressmen were extremely touchy.

The story of Erie Basin Metal Products, the Garsson brothers, and Andrew J. May is one of the more disturbing cases of the war, involving as it did the misuse of the chairmanship of the House Military Affairs Committee for personal gain. The story was told for the record during the summer of 1946 at a series of hearings held by the Truman Committee, of which Senator Mead was then chairman. May refused to appear in response to a subpoena, and a heart attack saved him from a later scheduled voluntary appearance. After his defeat in the election of 1946, and Senator Kilgore's succession to the chairmanship of the Committee, the matter was dropped; Kilgore concluded, as one observer put it, "with a phrase which seemed to make a mockery of committee procedure and two thousand pages of testimony: 'There is no evidence that May ever got a cent.' " [13]

In December, 1946, the Committee investigated the relations of Senator Bilbo with certain war contractors. The investigation was thorough and penetrating. A forthright report was issued to the Senate that doubtless played a part in the Senate's postponement of his seating in January, 1947. The Committee reported:

> The evidence presented to this committee clearly indicates that Senator Bilbo improperly used his high office as United States Senator for his personal gain in his dealings with war contractors. . . .
> The committee considers Senator Bilbo's acceptance of expensive gifts and donations of personal property and the acceptance of improvements to real estate, provided by contractors who have profited out of their work for the Government in the war effort, to be an illegal practice in violation of existing Federal statutes.[14]

The only investigation of a member of Congress during Truman's chairmanship involved "Happy" Chandler's swimming pool. On July 1, 1942, Senator Albert B. Chandler, a Kentucky Democrat, requested the Truman Committee to investigate certain charges being made by a political opponent named John Young Brown that Chandler had received a swimming pool from a war contractor for his services in obtaining contracts. The Committee was not anxious to take on the investigation, but Matthew Connelly, probably the most politically astute member of the staff, was sent to investigate. On the basis of his investigation the Committee reported to the Senate on July 16, "the committee has found no evidence and Mr. Brown has supplied no evidence in any way indicating that Senator Chandler interceded with anyone to assist Mr. Collins or his companies to obtain any contracts." [15] No mention was made of the propriety or impropriety of a Senator's accepting a swimming pool from a contractor who was doing business with the government. The report closed the incident, and one can imagine that the Committee members (especially the Democrats) heaved a sigh of relief, for as Republican member Joseph H. Ball later put it, " 'Happy' Chandler was a well-liked member of the 'club' and Harry was on the spot. None of us would have wanted to hurt 'Happy'." [16]

The investigations involving members of Congress were among the poorest conducted by the Committee because it "ducked" the issues except in the case of Senator Bilbo (and he was in Senatorial disfavor for other reasons). The Committee was willing to put the facts on record, but it was unwilling or unable to go further. Had it done so its relations with Congress undoubtedly would have suffered, for this was an area which most members of Congress preferred to leave untouched. The Committee accepted the "club" tradition and avoided the issue of proper relations between Congressmen and war contractors.

THE COMMITTEE'S ACHIEVEMENTS

Senator Truman, the first chairman of the Committee, resigned on August 4, 1944 after receiving the Democratic Party's nomination for the Vice-Presidency. His service as chairman extended over about half of the Committee's existence. During this period the Committee issued thirty-two of its fifty-one reports and accumulated twenty-four of its volumes of public hearings. Much of the subsequent work of the Committee dealt with issues and problems already under consideration before Truman's departure, and the Committee's procedures and role had been established. Jonathan Daniels reports one harsh judgment: "Three months after Truman left, according to a man above all others who should know, 'it had gone to the dogs.' " Daniels's own judgment is more moderate and eminently fair: "When Truman left the basic idea did not depart but the committee's accomplishment was completed." [17]

By 1944, when Truman left, the major problems of the industrial mobilization had been solved or the solutions were in sight. Ultimate victory seemed assured. The Committee was turning more and more to problems of reconversion from war to peace; less and less of its efforts were directed at remedying shortages of materials, equipment, and productive facilities, and more and more attention was directed at cases of fraud or corruption. And with the shifting emphasis came greater confusion in definition of the public interest. Whatever the differences about the means to achieve it, and however many persons subordinated it to their own interests, winning the war constituted a common goal which faded with the approach of peace. Uninhibited self-seeking then became the accepted pattern of behavior. The change was naturally reflected in Congress and in the activities of the Truman Committee.

An example of the Committee's changing attitudes is found in its concern with renegotiation. In the summer of 1941, the Committee discovered excessive profits accruing to shipbuilders. In its First Annual Report the Committee expressed severe criticism of Navy contracting, quoting one contractor as having said, "If it hadn't been for taxes, we couldn't have handled our profits with a steam shovel." [18] The Committee strongly recommended a procedure for contract review to protect the government's financial interests more effectively than tax policy could. The result of this suggestion, together with the investigations of other committees and a general Congressional concern with the prevention of war profiteering, led to the enactment of the Renegotiation Act of 1942. The Committee took a proprietary interest in the operation of this controversial piece of legislation, holding several hearings on its operation and taking credit for its adoption.

It is beyond the scope of this study to evaluate renegotiation. As a profit-limiting measure, it succeeded in recovering about one-fourth of the before-tax profits on war contracts [19] thereby preventing postwar scandals. Still, one study found that the "return on beginning net worth during war years far exceeded previous experience." [20] As a pricing device, the measure was not effectively used to encourage and reward efficiency, a fault not of the act but of its administration.[21]

Although renegotiation was a Congressional measure, and Congress was strongly in favor of strict limitation of profits in theory, Congressional concern recentered on the protection of constituents from excessive zeal on the part of administrators. The Truman Committee's emphasis changed also. Its Fourth Annual Report of July 30, 1945, while still claiming credit for a good law, was more concerned with suspending renegotiation at the end of 1945 than it was in evaluating the law in terms of its objectives.[22]

A year after Truman left the Committee the war ended, and the rapid demobilization thereafter left the Committee little to do except to rake up scandals and conduct post-mortem investigations. There was little public interest in these matters, which were rapidly becoming "ancient history," for people's efforts were directed toward getting back to normal as quickly as possible. So it does not seem unfair to say that the Committee's mission was essentially completed by the time Truman resigned. This study, therefore, has concentrated on the Committee's activities during the Truman period.

Although no detailed balance sheet of the Committee's accomplishments is possible, for some of them consist of intangibles, the major contributions of the Truman Committee to the war effort seem to be:

1. *Its role as "trouble-shooter" of the war effort.* Although its contributions in this role are impossible to inventory precisely, during its first two or three years the Committee played a vital role which *Time* aptly described as "the closest thing yet to a domestic high command." [23] During this period its efforts to secure effective coordination of the war effort and its mediation of disputes between agencies made the Truman Committee a powerful force in the attainment of a functioning mobilization program. Some of its important work in this area is still unknown, for its influence was often exerted in private meetings, without hearings or publicity. Perhaps an adequate assessment was made by the anonymous Washingtonian who commented in 1943, "There's only one thing that worries me more than the present state of the war effort. That's to think what it would be like by now without TRUMAN." [24]

2. *The enormous monetary savings it effected.* Estimates of these savings run as high as $15 billion. This estimate may well be too high, but there is no doubt that the total savings in cost of war goods effected by the Committee runs into the billions of dollars—and constitutes a gratifying return on the investment of less than a million dollars in the Committee's work. This contribution is often exaggerated in importance, however, for it is an artificial measure of the Committee's total worth.

3. *The lessening of graft and corruption.* There is no way of knowing how great was the deterrent effect of possible Commit-

tee investigation on governmental officials, shady contractors, and influence peddlers. There is no reason to believe that this effect was insubstantial, and the relatively few cases of graft and outright corruption discovered after the war supports the conclusion that the Committee forced higher standards on contractors and contracting officers than would have been the case in its absence.

4. *Its role as a major source of information about the war program.* There was a tendency among most of the officials of wartime Washington to divulge as little as possible of their activities to the public. In some measure this was a result of necessary security considerations, and in part it was due to the pressures of the war, which pushed public information into the background. But it was also due to a desire to give a picture of the progress of the war that could be used to manipulate the public to do what was wanted. And secrecy was also used to protect officials from criticism of mistakes and bungling. The Truman Committee constantly exerted pressure upon public officials, both civilian and military, to give the public maximum information about the conduct of the war at home and abroad and forced them to justify withholding of information. The Committee itself was a major source of information about the war, although it stayed well within the limits imposed by security considerations. The contributions of the Truman Committee toward greater public knowledge of the conduct of the war were incalculable.

5. *Its contribution to public confidence in the conduct of the war.* The average citizen was remote from the conduct of the war abroad and from the operation of the mobilization program in Washington. Many people were close to some segment of the war program in their own communities, however, and frequently they were disturbed by things they saw which they did not understand or which really did need correction. The Truman Committee was not, of course, able to allay all suspicions, but its func-

tion as an agency to which any citizen could carry his complaints or doubts and receive a reasonable answer contributed significantly to public confidence in the conduct of the domestic side of the war effort. Many complaints received by the Committee were without foundation, and a letter of explanation was sent to the complainant. Others were justified, and investigation resulted in correction. Even when the Committee was publicly critical of some phase of mobilization, its over-all evaluation was usually favorable—pointing out that most officials were honestly trying to do a good job. This further contributed to public confidence. And the information the Committee provided about the war effort also contributed to the maintenance of public confidence in the governmental leadership.

6. *Its impact on the military.* The Committee prodded the military to do its job, but at the same time constantly exerted pressure on the military to stay within the limits of that job and to minimize encroachment upon civilian responsibility. The Committee was a major force working on behalf of legitimate civilian needs throughout the war. This was not, however, an interference with military needs. The evidence of World War II does not suggest that giving the military everything it asks for produces either maximum or balanced production. Much of the evidence suggests the contrary.

There were substantial differences in the administration of the Services that were reflected in the Committee's relations with them. Navy procurement was under the control of Under Secretary James V. Forrestal, who exercised an independent judgment and effective control over the Navy's industrial mobilization. While he was a vigorous advocate of the Navy's needs and never admitted Navy errors if it could be avoided, he recognized the authority of the WPB and was sophisticated in his understanding of the complexities of the economy and the legitimacy of other claims besides those of the Navy. Furthermore the Navy (and Forrestal) was more sensitive to public opinion, and hence more responsible in the correction of mistakes before it was necessary to admit them in public. While Forrestal may have preferred that Congressional committees leave him alone, he recognized the necessary role of Congress and appears to have genuinely believed that the Truman Committee's work was constructive, as he indicated to Truman:

> The Truman committee has served a useful purpose in providing a medium for the exploration of criticisms of the war effort. Its work has been as objective as I think it possible for such investigations to be, and both committee and counsel have endeavored to conserve the time of witnesses. The tempo at which this war is being waged and the resulting need of speed of accomplishment mean there should be constant review and survey, particularly of the procurement side of the war effort. The Navy has this constantly in mind and is, therefore, conducting a continuous scrutiny of its business operations. In the vast area being covered by its operations, however, and the greatly increased scope of its business it welcomes the kind of additional outside scrutiny which your committee has given.[25]

Such was not the case with Under Secretary of War Robert P. Patterson, who was in charge of both Army and Air Force procurement. Absolutely selfless in his devotion to the national interest as he saw it, he tended to identify this interest with the Army's interests. He was dedicated to winning the war before anything else, and this inclined him to see policy differences in terms of patriotism and morality. His sense of dedication also led him on occasion to justify the means by the ends. Thus Patterson became an advocate of the Army, right or wrong, and failed to exercise effective control over the procurement program. It is probable that a stronger individual who tried to exercise control would have had great difficulty with General Somervell, but Patterson's role produced little friction. Tending to recognize, in practice, no claims but those dictated by his concept of military necessity, he constantly fought the authority of the War Production Board, which he felt was being exerted on behalf of a civilian population which would not sacrifice for the sake of the war. Thus he could defend the Canol Project as a strategic necessity while he opposed the manufacture of spare parts to keep the transportation system of the country functioning.

These differences in character and temperament were reflected in the relations of the Services with the Truman Committee. Before he took the position of chief counsel to the Committee, Hugh Fulton contacted both men, Patterson in person and Forrestal through John Cahill, who acted for him as attorney. Patterson promised Fulton that he would cooperate fully with him and urged him to undertake the job. But Forrestal told Fulton that he would not guarantee cooperation in advance. During the Committee's life, however, Patterson repeatedly obstructed its work and was often less than completely honest with it. Forrestal, on the other hand, did cooperate with the Committee and was honest; Fulton found that he could accept any statement of Forrestal's at face value.[26]

The Truman Committee shared the traditional American distrust of the military, although it was generous in its praise when it found military personnel who did not fit the expected pattern. The Committee saw the military mind as rigid, shortsighted, and ignorant of the complexities of the economy. It saw itself as an instrument for helping to shake the military loose from "hidebound" ways of doing things and as an instrument for helping to keep the insatiable demands of the military within reasonable bounds. It resisted the demands, not out of a desire to protect the civilian or merely to save money, but because it regarded the services as slow, inefficient, and incredibly wasteful when they entered fields other than those concerned with military matters. The conviction that the military lacked understanding of the economy was deepened by the persistent response from Patterson and Somervell, in particular, that "in war money is no object," and by the Committee's inability to convince them that money merely represented scarce materials and manpower. The Committee wanted the armed services to give realistic lists of their requirements to the WPB; the latter would then balance these needs with the basic civilian needs within the capabilities of the economy and provide the goods. The Services could then get on with fighting the war. The Committee was, of course, never successful in keeping the military within these limits, nor did it regard these limits as attainable under existing conditions.

It has been pointed out that the Truman Committee's political success—its unanimous reports, its high standing on both sides of the aisle, its prestige with very broad segments of the public—was due to the fact that it appealed to both factions of the Democratic Party and to Republicans as well. Its criticisms of defense agencies pleased the conservative, anti-Administration Democrats and the Republicans, and its criticisms of the military pleased the New Dealers.[27] But its appeal was broader than that.

It is certainly true that the Committee's criticisms of the defense agencies pleased Administration critics. Senator Arthur H. Vandenberg, in particular, frequently tried to personalize the blame, as for example in this exchange:

Mr. Vandenberg. In other words, the Senator is now saying that the chief bottleneck which the defense program confronts is the lack of adequate organization and coordination in the administration of defense?

Mr. Truman. That is exactly what the hearings before our committee will prove.

Mr. Vandenberg. Who is responsible for that situation?

Mr. Truman. There is only one place where the responsibility can be put.

Mr. Vandenberg. Where is that—the White House?

Mr. Truman.   Yes, sir.

Mr. Vandenberg.   I thank the Senator. (Laughter).[28]

Or this one:

Mr. Brewster.   So we are seeking to bring to the attention of the proper authorities any irregularity which would seem to warrant further action.

Mr. Vandenberg.   Has anything happened to anyone as a result?

Mr. Brewster.   Some have gone to jail, I think, but not in sufficient numbers yet to satisfy either the requirements of the situation or possibly the sadistic desires of the Senator from Michigan. (Laughter).[29]

And it is true that Committee criticisms of the military pleased New Dealers. But its criticisms were frequently based on home-front considerations which the Committee believed were being neglected by the military—a feeling that was shared by many Congressmen who were not New Dealers. Furthermore, the Committee's long advocacy of spreading contracts geographically and among smaller producers had the support of virtually all Congressmen. A very important element in the Truman Committee's political success was this ability to give voice to civilian needs and concerns within the framework of a national interest directed at winning the war.

A RESPONSIBLE COMMITTEE

It will be recalled that in the Introduction six criteria for judging the responsibility of Congressional investigating committees were suggested. These criteria were:

1. Does the committee reflect some concept of the "public interest" rather than the personal economic, political, or sectional interests of its chairman and members?

2. Are its criticisms constructive rather than destructive?

3. Does the committee emphasize fairly broad policy considerations, rather than minute details, and does it exercise re-

straint in substituting its judgment for that of the responsible administrative officials?

4. Does the committee use its great power for influencing public opinion responsibly, sticking to demonstrable facts and presenting them honestly and fairly, but at the same time searching out the full facts with thoroughness and vigor?

5. Does the committee stay within the limits of its mission?

6. Are its methods of operation fair to those who come under its scrutiny?

It will also be recalled that it was suggested that the pragmatic standard of an investigating committee's success is likely to be its political effectiveness. By that standard the Truman Committee's success is eloquently attested by the rise to political prominence of its first chairman. Many astute political observers in wartime Washington expected the chief figure in the war mobilization program to become the leading vice-presidential candidate in 1944. They looked for Nelson to assume this role, and there were some moves on his behalf. But, partly because of Nelson's difficulties and partly because of the Committee's effectiveness, Truman became the chief figure of the domestic side of the war effort and became the Democratic nominee in spite of Roosevelt's lack of enthusiasm for him.

As far as the six criteria enumerated above go, there would seem to be a higher degree of agreement with the judgment that the Truman Committee met them successfully than there is with most Congressional committees. The Truman Committee met none of these standards perfectly, but on balance it gets a favorable answer to each of the questions, particularly when the scrutiny is confined to the period of Truman's chairmanship, thus:

1. The Truman Committee managed to submerge the particular interests of its members uncommonly well, and it exhibited a rare degree of agreement upon a concept of "public interest"

to govern its work. Only rarely did parochial or personal interests of individual members intrude on the Committee's work. The members conceived the public interest to lie in speedy and economical victory, which would be best achieved, they believed, with centralized and effective control of the mobilization program, balanced production, adequate consideration of essential civilian needs, minimization of waste, elimination of fraud, and high quality in the goods produced.

2. In general, the Committee's criticisms were constructive. It avoided "scapegoating" and was usually careful not to impugn the motives of those it criticized. Even when it was quite critical of agencies in the executive branch, it sought to protect their over-all reputation. Consequently, its findings were usually accorded respect, even when there was strong disagreement with them. Its practice of submitting advance copies of reports to those affected is clear evidence that it preferred accuracy to sensational headlines.

3. The Truman Committee was about as successful in exerting its influence on the domestic aspects of the war program as any investigating committee could have been. It lacked the standing committees' important power to report out legislation, but in spite of this the Committee did influence some important pieces of legislation during its life. Its primary mission was to check on the administration of the war program, to ensure adherence to established Congressional and Administration policies, and to secure a clear-cut policy where there was none. Unfortunately, there were some important issues on which a clearly defined policy was lacking, notably with respect to the organization of production and procurement. The Truman Committee was never satisfied with the solutions to this problem, which it regarded as a crucial one. Where there was not an established policy the Committee's role was difficult, for it tried to restrain itself from substituting its judgment for that of the responsible

administrative agencies. The Committee largely limited itself to prodding the agencies to establish a policy and to indicating what lines it thought the policy should take. For example, although the Committee differed with Nelson on the use of dollar-a-year men, it did not push the issue when Nelson determined *his* position. The Committee was more concerned with broad policy than with this relatively unimportant detail.

In this respect, the Truman Committee was in some ways unique. In contrast to the prevalent Congressional-Executive antagonism, the Truman Committee had sought active cooperation with the President—it had tried to "help the President win the war." In contrast to the more common Congressional tendency to splinter authority and weaken executive power, the Truman Committee had exerted every effort to secure effective coordination and tight executive control of a highly centralized mobilization organization. In fact, the Committee had gone further in this direction than Roosevelt himself had desired. Its reasons for doing so are still not entirely clear, for in its reports the Committee usually justified its position by saying that tighter control was necessary to end the confusion and win the war. The Committee hoped that more effective control would reduce the friction that characterized relations among the war agencies. This was certainly an important reason for its position, but there were others. Probably most important was the Committee's belief that only strong central control could withstand military demands for the sacrifice of everything civilian. The Committee was convinced that civilian needs would fall before a military onslaught unless there was a civilian agency strong enough to enforce its decisions on the military. It felt that decisions in the agency had to be made by one man, not a board that the military could dominate.

4. Congressional investigations are essentially exercises in the creation of public opinion. The facts an investigating committee

digs up are usually, although not always, fairly widely known. The function of the committee is to put them on the public record—usually in a manner calculated to get maximum public attention. The Truman Committee sometimes discovered information unknown to the responsible officials, but this was the exception. Usually it was the public disclosure, or often the prospective disclosure, which brought action. Holding up to public view the actions of administrators is an extremely important function of Congress; in a government of divided powers it is vital if the legislature is to retain any control over administration.

The Truman Committee searched out facts with vigor and utilized its opportunities to put them before the public, but presented them fairly and honestly. Rarely did those to whom reports were sent before publication find substantial errors of fact or complain about fairness—although they often differed on interpretation.

5. The Truman Committee's mandate was so broad that it had little difficulty staying within its mission. The major limit— staying away from matters of military strategy and tactics—was carefully observed. In fact, perhaps on occasion the Committee was too scrupulous, permitting the armed services to protect themselves from scrutiny by labeling "strategic" what was not— the Canol Project, for example. And the Committee deferred to standing committees whenever they indicated a desire to study a situation within their purview.

Two further reasons why the Truman Committee avoided jurisdictional friction within Congress are that many of the matters it dealt with were not clearly within the jurisdiction of particular standing committees of Congress, and that only one of the four wartime Congressional committees for the armed services—the House Naval Affairs Committee—was effective during the war years. Consequently, the Committee had a relatively clear field, to which it had little difficulty confining itself.

6. The Committee's procedures were discussed in detail in Chapter 2. Not only do they seem fair to an outside observer, but they were regarded as fair by most of those who were subjected to Committee scrutiny. The fact that the Committee offered a forum where any agency could get a fair hearing (as could an individual if he had a pertinent reason) served to mollify many whom the Committee touched with its criticism and enhanced its reputation as a responsible agency of Congress.

In short, the Truman Committee became a responsible committee through the exercise of restraint. Off-hand, this may not appear to be a very effusive accolade. But, given prior experience with Congressional investigations and that to come in the 1950's, the Truman Committee's performance was an impressive demonstration of the potential of a responsible committee when it does exercise restraint. Through its example the Committee enhanced the influence and prestige of Congress and set a high standard against which subsequent committees may be judged.

Notes

INTRODUCTION: NOTES

1 *Congressional Government* (Boston: Houghton Mifflin, 15th impression, 1900), p. 303.
2 M. Nelson McGeary, "Congressional Investigations: Historical Development," *The University of Chicago Law Review*, XVIII (1951), p. 425.
3 Telford Taylor, *Grand Inquest* (New York: Simon & Schuster, 1955), pp. 23–24. Taylor has an excellent treatment of the history of investigating committees and of judicial restraints upon them.
4 *Ibid.*, chapters III and IV.
5 The major cases are Kilbourn v. Thompson, 103 U.S. 168 (1881); U.S. v. Rumely, 345 U.S. 41 (1953); and Watkins v. United States, 354 U.S. 178 (1957).
6 *American Democracy and Military Power* (Chicago: University of Chicago Press, 1951), p. 172.
7 *Ibid.*, p. 203.
8 *Ibid.*, pp. 211–12.

CHAPTER 1: NOTES

1 *Congressional Record*, August 3, 1944, p. 6747 (all references are to the permanent edition of the *C.R.*).
2 Jonathan Daniels, *The Man of Independence* (Philadelphia: J. B. Lippincott, 1950), pp. 218–19. Also Frank McNaughton and Walter Hehmeyer, *This Man Truman* (New York: McGraw-Hill, 1945).

3 William P. Helm, *Harry Truman: A Political Biography* (New York: Duell, Sloan & Pearce, 1947), p. 152.

4 *C.R.*, February 10, 1941, pp. 830, 838.

5 Helm, *op. cit.*, p. 159.

6 Daniels, *op. cit.*, p. 223.

7 *Ibid.*, pp. 222–23.

8 Samuel Lubell, *The Future of American Politics* (New York: Harper & Bros., 1952), p. 16.

9 *C.R.*, January 13, 1941, p. 138.

10 Lubell, *op. cit.*, p. 16.

11 *Ibid.*, p. 17. Lubell's source of information was probably Byrnes or an intimate of Byrnes's.

12 *C.R.*, March 1, 1941, p. 1615. When Cox's resolution was brought to the floor of the House on March 11 it was rejected largely because of the opposition of the Committee on Military Affairs and the fears of many Congressmen that it would be an anti-labor investigation. *C.R.*, March 11, 1941, pp. 2182–90.

13 *C.R.*, March 1, 1941, p. 1615. For the text of Sen. Res. 71 see Appendix I.

14 U.S. Congress, Senate, Special Committee Investigating the National Defense Program, *Final Report*, Sen. Report 440, Part 6, 80th Cong., 2d Sess. (Washington: Government Printing Office, 1948), p. 13. The Committee issued five annual reports and a final report, in each of which were reprinted the interim reports issued since the previous annual report, in chronological order and with continuous pagination. A list of these reports will be found in Appendix IV. Citations hereafter will refer first to the original report by number, and secondly, in parentheses, to the annual report in which it is reprinted. The page reference is to the annual report. Example above: R. 440, Pt. 6 (Final Report), p. 13.

15 Daniels, *op. cit.*, p. 223.

16 R. 440, Pt. 6 (Final Report), p. 13. A list of Senate resolutions affecting the Committee will be found in Appendix I.

17 Stephen K. Bailey and Howard D. Samuel, *Congress at Work* (New York: Holt, 1952), p. 297.

18 Personal interviews with staff members. See bibliography.

19 Wesley McCune and John R. Beal, "The Job That Made Truman President," *Harper's*, June, 1945, p. 617.

20 Daniels, *op. cit.*, p. 223.

21 Bailey and Samuel, *op. cit.*, p. 299.

22 Quoted in Daniels, *op. cit.*, p. 298.

23 Hugh Fulton, personal interview.

24 For a list of the Committee's principal assistants see Appendix III.

25 Wilbur D. Sparks, personal interview.

26 Joseph Borkin, personal interview, and Rudolph Halley, interview.

27 *C.R.,* February 10, 1941, p. 837.

28 Daniels, *op. cit.,* pp. 217–18; Truman, personal interview.

29 R. 10, Pt. 9 (3rd Annual), p. 333.

30 *C.R.,* December 10, 1941, pp. 9600–01.

31 Report of Senator Harry S Truman on findings of Committee (2nd Annual), p. 220.

32 Truman, personal interview.

33 Reprinted in 87 Cong. Rec. A3628 (1941).

34 R. 480, Pt. 5 (1st Annual), p. 3.

35 Report of Senator Harry S Truman on findings of Committee (2nd Annual), pp. 217–20.

36 R. 10, Pt. 9 (3rd Annual), p. 334.

CHAPTER 2: NOTES

1 *Congressional Record,* January 15, 1942, p. 390.

2 Stephen K. Bailey and Howard D. Samuel, *Congress at Work* (New York: Holt, 1952), p. 294.

3 Jerry Voorhis, "Congressional Investigations: Inner Workings," *University of Chicago Law Review,* XVIII (Spring, 1951), p. 460.

4 Jonathan Daniels, *The Man of Independence* (Philadelphia: J. B. Lippincott, 1950), p. 226.

5 Truman, personal interview.

6 *Hearings,* Pt. 6, p. 1663.

7 Colonel Frank B. Jordan, head of the Congressional Investigations Division of the Office of Legislative Liaison, interview, Washington, D.C. Col. Jordan made available copies of the relevant War Department orders.

8 Miles Knowles, personal interview.

9 William S. Abell, personal interview. Abell was an assistant to Nash.

10 Wilbur D. Sparks, personal interview.

11 See *Infra,* Chap. 3.

12 Joseph Borkin, personal interview. Borkin was an assistant to Wendell Berge in the Anti-Trust Division.

13 The facts in the remainder of this chapter were developed from interviews with Committee members, staff members, and other observers of the Committee, and from examination of the Committee's hearings and reports. They were checked with three secondary sources. First, Matthew Yang, "The Truman Committee" (unpublished Ph.D. disserta-

tion, Department of Political Science, Harvard University, 1948). Yang worked with the staff of the Committee for several months. His dissertation has a brief history of the Committee, a descriptive chapter on procedures, and a long chapter summarizing the work of the Committee during the period of Truman's chairmanship. Second, Harry Aubrey Toulmin, *Diary of Democracy: The Truman Committee* (New York: Richard R. Smith, 1947), a journalistic and uncritical summary of the Committee's work with little attention to procedures. Third, and containing the best treatment of procedures, is Bailey and Samuel, *op. cit.*, chapter XI, Part 1. Since the information comes from many sources which are in substantial agreement, citation will not be made unless there is a single source for an item.

[14] *Hearings,* Pt. 17, p. 6786.
[15] Truman, personal interview.
[16] Frank McNaughton and Walter Hehmeyer, *This Man Truman* (New York: McGraw-Hill, 1945), pp. 101–02.
[17] "Memorandum of Salient Points in Connection with the Testimony of Mr. Nelson," Committee files in the National Archives.
[18] Wesley McCune and John R. Beal, "The Job That Made Truman President," *Harper's,* June, 1945, p. 618.
[19] *Hearings,* Pt. 18, pp. 7403–04.
[20] *Hearings,* Pt. 1, pp. 286–301.
[21] Joseph H. Ball, personal interview.
[22] Agnes Straus Wolf, personal interview.
[23] McNaughton and Hehmeyer, *op. cit.,* p. 111.

CHAPTER 3: NOTES

[1] *Hearings,* Pt. 10, p. 4028.
[2] James W. Fesler *et al., Industrial Mobilization for War* (Washington: Government Printing Office, 1947), pp. 4–5. A more detailed analysis of the Industrial Mobilization Plan is contained in Robert H. Connery, *The Navy and the Industrial Mobilization in World War II* (Princeton: Princeton University Press, 1951), Chap. 3.
[3] Eliot Janeway, *The Struggle for Survival* (New Haven: Yale University Press, 1951), p. 63.
[4] Fesler, *op. cit.,* p. 23.
[5] *Ibid.,* p. 24.
[6] *Ibid.,* pp. 35–36.
[7] *Hearings,* Pt. 1, p. 19.
[8] *Ibid.,* p. 108.

9 *Minutes of the Council of the Office of Production Management,* War Production Board Documentary Publication No. 2 (Washington: Government Printing Office, 1946), p. 21.

10 Fesler, *op. cit.,* p. 147.

11 *Ibid.,* p. 121.

12 *Ibid.*

13 *Ibid.,* p. 145.

14 *Hearings,* Pt. 6, p. 1608.

15 *Hearings,* Pt. 7, pp. 2076–78.

16 For example see the case of the American Bantam Car Co., which had done "pioneering work" in the development of the jeep but was bypassed when mass orders were placed. *Hearings,* Pt. 7.

17 Frank McNaughton and Walter Hehmeyer, *This Man Truman* (New York: McGraw-Hill, 1945), pp. 113–14. See also *Congressional Record,* Jan. 15, 1942, pp. 380ff.

18 R. 480, Pt. 5 (1st Annual), pp. 6–7.

19 *Ibid.,* pp. 7–10.

20 *Ibid.,* p. 4 (note).

21 Robert E. Sherwood, *Roosevelt and Hopkins* (New York: Harper, 1948), p. 475.

22 Byrnes, *Speaking Frankly* (New York: Harper, 1947), p. 16.

23 Donald M. Nelson, *Arsenal of Democracy* (New York: Harcourt, Brace, 1946), pp. 196–97. There is an apparent conflict in Nelson's account and Byrnes's. Byrnes believed that he, Hopkins, and Harold D. Smith were drafting the Executive Order setting up WPB; actually they prepared the announcement of January 13. See Sherwood, *op. cit.,* p. 475.

24 Executive Order 9040, printed in Samuel I. Rosenman, ed., *The Public Papers and Addresses of Franklin D. Roosevelt* (New York: Harper, 1950), 1942 Vol., pp. 54–56.

25 A balanced appraisal is found in Fesler, *op. cit.,* pp. 208–11.

26 *Ibid.,* p. 209.

27 *Ibid.,* p. 210.

28 *Ibid.,* p. 211.

29 *Hearings,* Pt. 10, p. 4028.

30 *Ibid.,* p. 4043.

31 *Ibid.,* p. 4030.

32 *Hearings,* Pt. 12. Executive hearings were also held.

33 R. 480, Pt. 8 (2nd Annual), pp. 79ff.

34 Letter, Nelson to Truman, June 16, 1942, Committee files in the National Archives.

35 Nelson, *op. cit.,* p. 198.

36 Truman, personal interview; Fulton, interview.

[37] Nelson, *op. cit.*, pp. 198–200.

[38] *Hearings,* Pt. 10, pp. 4050–51.

[39] Connery, *op. cit.*, p. 143.

[40] John D. Millett, *The Organization and Role of the Army Service Forces* (Washington: Government Printing Office, 1954), pp. 36–39.

[41] Janeway, *op. cit.*, pp. 305–06, states flatly that this was the case.

[42] A copy of the agreement with the War Department is reproduced in Millett, *op. cit.*, pp. 442–45.

[43] *Hearings,* Pt. 12, pp. 5076–77.

[44] *Ibid.*, pp. 5228–29.

[45] For comments on Somervell's personality and character see Millett, *op. cit.*, pp. 6–7, and William D. Leahy, *I Was There* (New York: McGraw-Hill, 1950), pp. 127, 130.

[46] Brehon B. Somervell, personal interview.

[47] *Ibid.* Hugh Fulton stated to the writer that he privately investigated this charge and did not believe it to be true, although there is no proof; it is Somervell's word against Truman's. It is interesting to note that Truman asked Somervell to head the Defense Production Authority during the Korean War; President Truman to General Somervell, letters in Somervell's possession.

[48] Fesler, *op. cit.*, p. 258.

[49] Quoted in Millett, *op. cit.*, pp. 197–98.

[50] Fesler, *op. cit.*, p. 228.

[51] 863rd Press Conference, November 24, 1942. Reprinted in Rosenman, *op. cit.*, pp. 489–90.

[52] Nelson, *op. cit.*, p. 385.

[53] Leahy, *op. cit.*, pp. 130–31.

[54] The letter is printed in Elliott Roosevelt, ed., *F.D.R.: His Personal Letters 1928–1945* (New York: Duell, Sloan, 1950), Vol. II, pp. 1396–97.

[55] 77th Congress, 2d Sess., House, Select Committee Investigating National Defense Migration, *Sixth Interim Report,* October 20, 1942 (Washington: Government Printing Office, 1942), pp. 9, 22.

[56] Reprinted in R. 10, Pt. 4 (2nd Annual), p. 218.

[57] *Ibid.*, pp. 6–7.

[58] R. 10, pt. 9 (3rd Annual), p. 337.

[59] Executive Order 9347, May 27, 1943. An account of the events leading up to this order is found in Herman Miles Somers, *Presidential Agency* (Cambridge: Harvard University Press, 1950), pp. 23–38.

[60] Fesler, *op. cit.*, p. 554.

[61] David Novick, Melvin L. Anshen, and William C. Truppner, *Wartime Production Controls* (New York: Columbia University Press, 1949), pp. 382–83.

[62] *Ibid.*, p. 388.

CHAPTER 4: NOTES

[1] Donald M. Nelson, *Arsenal of Democracy* (New York: Harcourt, Brace, 1946), p. 389. President Roosevelt made this remark to Nelson after Nelson fired Eberstadt.

[2] *Minutes of the War Production Board,* Jan. 20, 1942 to Oct. 9, 1945, Documentary Publication No. 3 (Washington: Government Printing Office, 1946), pp. 178–79.

[3] *New York Times,* January 26, 1943, p. 1.

[4] Quoted in James W. Fesler *et al., Industrial Mobilization for War* (Washington: Government Printing Office, 1947), p. 566.

[5] *New York Times,* April 22, 1943, p. 15.

[6] *New York Times,* April 25, 1943, p. 37.

[7] *Hearings,* Pt. 19, p. 7648.

[8] *Ibid.,* pp. 7677–78.

[9] *Ibid.,* p. 7690.

[10] *Ibid.,* pp. 7695–96.

[11] *Ibid.,* pp. 7699–7700.

[12] *Ibid.,* p. 7726.

[13] *Ibid.,* pp. 7728–29.

[14] *Ibid.,* p. 7735.

[15] *Ibid.,* p. 7737.

[16] R. 10, Pt. 9 (3rd Annual, p. 333).

[17] *Ibid.,* p. 334.

[18] *Ibid.,* p. 337.

[19] Rudolph Halley, personal interview.

[20] Press release, June 24, 1943, Committee files in the National Archives.

CHAPTER 5: NOTES

[1] *I Was There* (New York: McGraw-Hill, 1950), p. 127.

[2] *Hearings,* Pt. 22, pp. 9388, 9454. This volume of hearings constitutes a comprehensive record of the Canol Project up to June, 1944, containing most of the relevant documents in its appendices.

[3] *Ibid.,* pp. 9492, 9640.

[4] *Ibid.,* pp. 9842–43.

[5] *Ibid.,* p. 9843.

[6] Graham's testimony on all these points is found *Ibid.,* pp. 9381–9406, 9573–96.

[7] Knowles, personal interview.

[8] *Hearings*, Pt. 22, pp. 9680, 9687.

[9] This hypothesis is supported by Admiral Leahy's account of Somervell's enthusiastic description of the project to him. *I Was There*, p. 127.

[10] The letter is printed in *Hearings*, Pt. 22, pp. 9855–57.

[11] *Ibid.*, p. 9481.

[12] Printed in *Hearings*, Pt. 22, pp. 9889–90.

[13] *Ibid.*, p. 9528.

[14] *Ibid.*, p. 9531.

[15] *Ibid.*, p. 9552.

[16] *Ibid.*, p. 9890.

[17] *Ibid.*, p. 9865.

[18] *Ibid.*, pp. 9873–75.

[19] *Ibid.*, pp. 9875–76.

[20] *Ibid.*, p. 9878. He referred to both the Alcan Highway and the Canol Project in these terms.

[21] *Ibid.*, p. 9571.

[22] Knowles, personal interview.

[23] *Hearings*, Pt. 22, pp. 9900–01.

[24] See Admiral King's testimony in *Hearings*, Pt. 39, p. 22991.

[25] In January, 1944, these were made public and are printed in *Hearings*, Pt. 22.

[26] R. 110, Pt. 7 (5th Annual), p. 23.

[27] *Hearings*, Pt. 22, p. 9596.

[28] *Ibid.*, pp. 9605–06.

[29] *Ibid.*, p. 9680.

[30] R. 10, Pt. 14 (3rd Annual), p. 460.

[31] *Ibid.*, p. 460 (italics are the Committee's).

[32] See remarks of Senator Ferguson on the floor of the Senate, June 21, 1944, reprinted in *Hearings*, Pt. 22, pp. 9930–34.

[33] Hugh Fulton, personal interview. See his correspondence with Amberg in *Hearings*, Pt. 22, pp. 9924–29.

[34] *Ibid.*, p. 9934.

[35] R. 110, Pt. 7 (5th Annual), p. 25.

[36] *Ibid.*, p. 24.

[37] *Hearings*, Pt. 39, p. 22991.

[38] *Ibid.*, p. 23010.

[39] Richard L. Neuberger, "The Great Canol Fiasco," *American Mercury*, April, 1948, p. 421. During the war the late Senator Neuberger was aide to the Commanding General, Northwest Service Command.

[40] John D. Millett, *The Organization and Role of the Army Service Forces* (Washington: Government Printing Office, 1954), p. 394.

CHAPTER 6: NOTES

[1] Unidentified corporation president, quoted in Edwin H. Sutherland, *White Collar Crime* (New York: Dryden Press, 1949), p. 174.

[2] Harry S. Truman, speech, "The Fight for Quality Production," printed in 89th Cong. Rec. A4146.

[3] R. 10, Pt. 10 (3rd Annual), p. 358.

[4] *Ibid.*, p. 359.

[5] *Ibid.*, p. 360.

[6] *Ibid.*

[7] *Ibid.*

[8] *Ibid.*, pp. 361–62.

[9] *Ibid.*, p. 362.

[10] *Ibid.*, p. 363.

[11] Miles H. Knowles, personal interview.

[12] *Ibid.*

[13] R. 10, Pt. 10 (4th Annual), pp. 364–65.

[14] *Ibid.*, p. 365.

[15] *Ibid.*, pp. 365–66.

[16] R. 10, Pt. 10 (3rd Annual), p. 366.

[17] *Ibid.*, p. 368.

[18] *Ibid.*, p. 366.

[19] *Ibid.*, p. 367.

[20] *New York Times,* July 11, 1943, p. 24.

[21] *Ibid.*

[22] For example see the editorial in the *New York Times,* July 12, 1943. One of the full-page ads appeared in the *Times* on July 14, 1943.

[23] *Hearings,* Pt. 20, pp. 8365–66.

[24] *Ibid.*, p. 8373, and *New York Times,* August 21, 1943, p. 6.

[25] *Hearings,* Pt. 20, pp. 8371–72.

[26] *Ibid.*, pp. 8375–76.

[27] *Ibid.*, p. 8380.

[28] *Ibid.*

[29] *Ibid.*, p. 8384.

[30] *Ibid.*, pp. 8393–94.

[31] Truman, "The Fight for Quality Production," *op. cit.*

[32] *Hearings,* Pt. 20, p. 8397.

[33] *Ibid.*, p. 8399.

[34] R. 10, Pt. 10 (3rd Annual), pp. 356–57.

[35] *Hearings,* Pt. 20, p. 8403.

[36] Truman, "The Fight for Quality Production," *op. cit.*

37 Both letters are reproduced in R. 110, Pt. 3 (4th Annual), pp. 299–300.
38 R. 110, Pt. 3 (4th Annual), p. 292.
39 *Hearings,* Pt. 30, p. 14471.
40 R. 110, Pt. 3 (4th Annual), p. 292.
41 *Ibid.,* p. 294.
42 Sutherland, *op. cit.,* p. 175.
43 This episode is documented in memoranda and exchanges of letters in the Committee files in the National Archives, where there is also a copy of the Truman speech.

CHAPTER 7: NOTES

1 *Congressional Government* (Boston: Houghton Mifflin, 15th impression, 1900), p. 299.
2 R. 440, Pt. 6 (Final Report), pp. 8–9.
3 U.S. Congress, House of Representatives, Military Affairs Committee, *Interim General Report,* House Report No. 2272, 77th Cong., 2nd Sess. (Washington: Government Printing Office, 1942), pp. 215, 259.
4 R. 480, Pt. 1 (1st Annual), p. 202.
5 R. 480, Pt. 7 (2nd Annual), p. 49.
6 *Ibid.,* p. 78.
7 R. 480, Pt. 5 (1st Annual), p. 172.
8 "Billion Dollar Watchdog," *Time,* March 8, 1943, reprinted in 89 *C.R.* 1560.
9 R. 480, Pt. 5 (1st Annual), p. 166.
10 See testimony of Lindsay Warren, Comptroller General of the U.S., *Hearings,* Pt. 35, pp. 19145, 19172.
11 *Hearings,* Pt. 18, p. 7215.
12 See H. H. Wilson, *Congress: Corruption and Compromise* (New York: Rinehart, 1951), Chap. 3, and *Hearings,* Pt. 35.
13 Wilson, *op. cit.,* p. 169. Also see *Hearings,* Pts. 34–35.
14 R. 110, Pt. 8 (Final Report), pp. 116, 122.
15 R. 480, Pt. 10 (2nd Annual), p. 115.
16 Joseph H. Ball, personal interview.
17 Daniels, *The Man of Independence* (Philadelphia: J. B. Lippincott Co., 1950), p. 227.
18 R. 480, Pt. 5 (1st Annual), p. 88.
19 Richard C. Osborn, *The Renegotiation of War Profits,* Bulletin 67 (Urbana: University of Illinois Bureau of Economic and Business Research, 1948), p. 79.
20 *Ibid.,* p. 92.

21 *Ibid.,* p. 93, and John P. Miller, *The Pricing of Military Procurements* (New Haven: Yale University Press, 1949), pp. 181 ff.

22 R. 110, Pt. 4 (4th Annual), pp. 24–25.

23 "Billion Dollar Watchdog," *op. cit.,* p. 1560.

24 Quoted, *Ibid.*

25 James V. Forrestal, Letter to Senator Truman, January 6, 1943.

26 Hugh Fulton, letter to the writer. See also Stephen K. Bailey and Howard D. Samuel, *Congress at Work* (New York: Henry Holt & Co., 1952), p. 309.

27 Samuel Lubell, *The Future of American Politics* (New York: Harper & Bros., 1952), p. 17.

28 *Congressional Record,* Aug. 14, 1941, pp. 7117–18.

29 *C.R.,* Jan. 15, 1942, p. 387.

APPENDIX I

S. Res. 71,   77th Congress, 1st sess.,   Mar. 1, 1941.[1]   *"Resolved,
that a special committee of seven Senators, to be appointed
by the President of the Senate, is authorized and directed to
make a full and complete study and investigation of the
operation of the program for the procurement and construction of supplies, materials, munitions, vehicles, aircraft, vessels, plants, camps, and other articles and facilities in connection with the national defense, including (1)
the types and terms of contracts awarded on behalf of the
United States; (2) the methods by which such contracts are
awarded and contractors selected; (3) the utilization of the
facilities of small business concerns, through subcontracts
or otherwise; (4) the geographic distribution of contracts
and location of plants and facilities; (5) the effect of such
program with respect to labor and the migration of labor;
(6) the performance of contracts and the accountings required of contractors; (7) benefits accruing to contractors
with respect to amortization for the purposes of taxation
or otherwise; (8) practices of management or labor, and
prices, fees, and charges, which interfere with such program or unduly increase its cost; and (9) such other matters
as the Committee deems appropriate. The Committee shall
report to the Senate, as soon as practicable, the results of
its study and investigation, together with its recommendations.*

*For purposes of this resolution the Committee, or any
duly authorized subcommittee thereof, is authorized to
hold such hearings, to sit and act at such times and places
during the sessions, recesses, and adjourned periods of the
Seventy-seventh and succeeding Congresses, to employ
such clerical and other assistance, to require by subpoena,
or otherwise, the attendance of such witnesses and the production of such correspondence, books, papers, and documents, to make such investigations, to administer such
oaths, to take such testimony, and to incur such expenditures as it deems advisable. The cost of stenographic serv-*

[1] S. Res. 71, which established the Committee and set forth its scope and
authority, is reprinted in full. All other resolutions are briefly summarized.

ices to report such hearings shall not be in excess of 25 cents per hundred words. The expenses of the Committee, which shall not exceed $15,000, shall be paid from the contingent fund of the Senate upon vouchers approved by the chairman of the committee."

S. Res. 112,   *77th Congress, 1st sess.,   May 6, 1941.*   Broadened scope to include investigation of defense plant locations.

S. Res. 146,   *77th Congress, 1st sess.,   August 11, 1941.*   Authorized use of the services, information, facilities, and personnel of executive branch of Government, and increased limit of expenditures.

S. Res. 175,   *77th Congress, 1st sess.,   Oct. 16, 1941.*   Increased membership to 10 Senators.

S. Res. 218,   *77th Congress, 2nd sess.,   Jan. 23, 1942.*   Increased limit of expenditures.

S. Res. 288,   *77th Congress, 2nd sess.,   Sept. 17, 1942.*   Ditto.

S. Res. 300,   *77th Congress, 2nd sess.,   Oct. 6, 1942.*   Broadened scope to include investigation of the gasoline-rationing program.

S. Res.   6,   *78th Congress, 1st sess.,   Jan. 25, 1943.*   Continued committee for the 78th Congress.

S. Res. 146,   *78th Congress, 1st sess.,   May 20, 1943.*   Increased limit of expenditures.

S. Res. 235,   *78th Congress, 2nd sess.,   Feb. 8, 1944.*   Ditto.

S. Res. 319,   *78th Congress, 2nd sess.,   Aug. 23, 1944.*   Ditto.

S. Res.   55,   *79th Congress, 1st sess.,   Jan. 29, 1945.*   Continued committee for the 79th Congress.

S. Res. 147,   *79th Congress, 1st sess.,   June 28, 1945.*   Increased limit of expenditures.

S. Res. 247,   *79th Congress, 2nd sess.,   April 1, 1946.*   Ditto.

S. Res. 309,   *79th Congress, 2nd sess.,   July 30, 1946.*   Ditto.

S. Res.   46,   *80th Congress, 1st sess.,   Jan. 22, 1947.*   Continued committee until Jan. 31, 1948, and limited scope to World World II.

S. Res.   89,   *80th Congress, 1st sess.,   Mar. 5, 1947.*   Increased limit of expenditures.

S. Res. 97,   *80th Congress, 1st sess.,   April 3, 1947.*   Limited application of certain provisions of Federal law to counsel of the committee.

S. Res. 107,   *80th Congress, 1st sess.,   May 23, 1947.*   Ditto.

S. Res. 145,   *80th Congress, 1st sess.,   July 23, 1947.*   Increased limit of expenditures.

APPENDIX II

Chairmen

Harry S Truman (Democrat, Missouri). Appointed chairman March 1, 1941; resigned Aug. 3, 1944.

James M. Mead (Democrat, New York). Appointed March 8, 1941; term in Senate expired Jan. 3, 1947; served as chairman from Aug. 11, 1944 to Oct. 1, 1946.

Harley M. Kilgore (Democrat, West Virginia). Appointed Nov. 27, 1941; resigned Jan. 24, 1947; served as chairman from Oct. 1, 1946 to Jan. 6, 1947.

Owen Brewster (Republican, Maine). Appointed March 8, 1941; named chairman of the Committee on Jan. 6, 1947.

Members

Joseph H. Ball (Republican, Minnesota). Appointed March 8, 1941; resigned March 12, 1947.

Styles Bridges (Republican, New Hampshire). Appointed Nov. 27, 1941; resigned March 16, 1942.

Frank Briggs (Democrat, Missouri). Appointed June 26, 1945; term in Senate expired Jan. 3, 1947.

Harold H. Burton (Republican, Ohio). Appointed March 16, 1942; resigned Sept. 30, 1945.

Harry P. Cain (Republican, Washington). Appointed Apr. 21, 1947.

Tom Connally (Democrat, Texas). Appointed March 8, 1941; resigned Jan. 24, 1947.

Homer Ferguson (Republican, Michigan). Appointed Jan. 28, 1943.

Carl A. Hatch (Democrat, New Mexico). Appointed Apr. 15, 1941; resigned June 26, 1945; reappointed Jan. 31, 1947.

Carl Hayden (Democrat, Arizona). Appointed March 8, 1941; resigned Apr. 15, 1941.

Clyde L. Herring (Democrat, Iowa). Appointed Nov. 27, 1941; term in Senate expired Jan. 3, 1943.

William F. Knowland (Republican, California). Appointed Oct. 29, 1945; resigned Apr. 21, 1947.

George W. Malone (Republican, Nevada). Appointed March 12, 1947.

Joseph R. McCarthy (Republican, Wisconsin). Appointed Jan. 24, 1947.

Hugh B. Mitchell (Democrat, Washington). Appointed March 6, 1945; resigned Dec. 26, 1946.

Herbert R. O'Conor (Democrat, Maryland). Appointed Jan. 31, 1947.

Claude Pepper (Democrat, Florida). Appointed Jan. 31, 1947.

James M. Tunnell (Democrat, Delaware). Appointed Aug. 10, 1944; term in Senate expired Jan. 3, 1947.

Mon C. Wallgren (Democrat, Washington). Appointed March 8, 1941; resigned Jan. 9, 1945.

John J. Williams (Republican, Delaware). Appointed Jan. 24, 1947.

APPENDIX III

Hugh A. Fulton. Appointed Chief Counsel on Mar. 31, 1941; resigned Sept. 15, 1944. Served previously as executive assistant to the United States attorney in the southern district of New York and as a special assistant to the Attorney General.

Charles Patrick Clark. Appointed associate chief counsel on Mar. 15, 1941; resigned Oct. 31, 1942. Served previously as assistant counsel and chief investigator on the Senate Interstate Commerce Committee. Also served on the Senate Committee on Education and Labor and other committees.

Rudolph Halley. Appointed executive assistant to the chief counsel on June 16, 1942. Named chief counsel on Sept. 15, 1944; resigned Sept. 28, 1945. Served previously as an assistant United States attorney for the southern district of New York.

George Meader. Appointed assistant counsel on July 1, 1943; named executive assistant to the chief counsel on Aug. 1, 1944, and appointed chief counsel on Oct. 1, 1945; resigned July 1, 1947. Served previously as prosecuting attorney of Washtenaw County, Ann Arbor, Michigan.

William P. Rogers. Appointed assistant counsel on Apr. 23, 1947, and named chief counsel on July 1, 1947. Served previously as an assistant district attorney in New York City.

Francis D. Flanagan. Appointed chief investigator on Jan. 1, 1945; named chief assistant counsel on Dec. 1, 1945. Served previously as special agent of the Federal Bureau of Investigation.

APPENDIX IV

[1] In each of the 5 annual reports and in the final report will be found reprints of the interim reports, except for R. 480, Pt. 4.

Part 8. Shipbuilding and Shipping. Apr. 22, 1943.
Part 9. Conflicting War Programs. May 6, 1943.
Part 10. Aircraft. July 10, 1943.
Part 11. Comparative Merits of Rayon and Cotton Tire Cord. July 16, 1943.
Part 12. Outlines of Problems of Conversion From War Production. Nov. 5, 1943.
Part 13. Transportation. Dec. 15, 1943.
Part 14. The Canol Project. Dec. 21, 1943.

Report No. 10 (78th Cong., 2nd sess.)

Part 15. Investigations Overseas; Section I—Petroleum Matters. Feb. 16, 1944.
Part 16. Third Annual Report. Mar. 4, 1944.
Part 17. Magnesium. Mar. 13, 1944.
Part 18. Merchant Shipping. June 23, 1944.
Part 19. Ream General Hospital. Aug. 22, 1944.
Part 20. Accumulation of Surpluses. Dec. 19, 1944.

Report No. 110 (79th Cong., 1st sess.)

Part 1. Disposal of Surpluses Other Than Industrial Plants. Mar. 22, 1945.
Part 2. Investigations Overseas. July 6, 1945.
Part 3. Aircraft—Conditions at Curtiss-Wright Corp., Buffalo, N.Y., Plants. July 26, 1945.
Part 4. Fourth Annual Report. July 30, 1945.

Report No. 110 (79th Cong., 2nd sess.)

Part 5. Investigations Overseas—Surplus Property Abroad. Mar. 22, 1946.
Part 6. Aircraft—Production, Development, and Research. June 7, 1946.
Part 7. Fifth Annual Report. Sept. 3, 1946.
Part 8. Transactions Between Senator Theodore G. Bilbo and Various War Contractors. Jan. 2, 1947.

Report No. 440 (80th Cong., 1st sess.)

Part 1. Inter-American Highway. July 7, 1947.

Report No. 440 (80th Cong., 2nd sess.)

Part 2. Renegotiation. Feb. 20, 1948.
Part 3. Aircraft—Hughes-Kaiser Flying Boat—Hughes Photo-Re-
connaissance Plane—Investigations Within the Air Forces.
Apr. 14, 1948.
Part 3a. Ditto—Minority Views. May 17, 1948.
Part 3b. Ditto—Additional Report. May 17, 1948.
Part 4. Industrial Mobilization for War. Apr. 28, 1948.
Part 4a. Ditto—Minority Views. May 18, 1948.
Part 5. Navy Purchases of Middle East Oil. Apr. 28, 1948 .
Part 6. Final Report. Apr. 28, 1948.

APPENDIX V

Manpower.
Reconversion program.
Army hotel acquisition program.
Part 22. September, October, November, December, 1943.
Canol Project.
Part 23. January, March, April, 1944.
Merchant shipping.
Part 24. March, May, June, 1944.
Magnesium.
Paper.
Corrigan, Osburne & Wells.
Reconversion.
Part 25. August, 1944.
Reconversion.
Disposal of surplus property.
Part 26. September, November, December, 1944.
Disposal of surplus property.
Manpower.
Reconversion.
Army inventory control.
World Wide Mercantile Corp.
Progress in war production.
Cigarette shortage.
Part 27. January, February, 1945.
Textile industry—manpower and production.
Disposal of surplus property—Surplus Liquidators, Inc.
Part 28. March, 1945.
Manpower problems in Detroit.
Part 29. May, June, 1945.
Carbon black.
Part 30. July, 1945.
Inspection at Curtiss-Wright Corp., Buffalo, N.Y., plants.
Part 31. July, August, 1945.
Reconversion.
Redeployment transportation.
Coal.
Aviation and light metals industries.
Part 32. September, October, November, December, 1945.
Tin shortage.
Disposal of surplus property—municipalities, veterans.
Reconversion.
Irregularities in Fourteenth Naval District.

APPENDIX VI

1942.
> February, March. Rubber.
> March. Shipbuilding.
> June. Tank lighters.
>> Barge transportation of oil.
> September. Manpower.
> October. Shipbuilding.
> December. Oil.

1943.
> January, February. Renegotiation.
> February, April, July. Barge and other oil shipments.
> February. Telenar press tool.
> February, March, April, May. Aviation—Wright Aeronautical Corp.
> March. Carnegie-Illinois Steel Co.
> April. Food waste.
>> Rubber tires.
>> Shipping.
>> Aviation—light metals.
> June. Helicopters.
>> Sunflower Ordnance Works.
>> Board of Economic Warfare.
> June, July, October, November. Overseas subcommittee.
> June, July, August, November. Aviation—aircraft.
> July, October, December. Transportation.
> July. Magnesium.
> August. Printing and Publishing Division, WPB.
> August. Curtiss-Wright Corp.
> September. Alcan Highway.
> September, October. Detroit tool sale.
> October. Brewster Aeronautical Corp.
>> Lockland Plant, Wright Aeronautical Corp.
>> Aviation—North American Aviation.
>> War Manpower Commission.
> October, November. Cramp Shipyard.
> October. Conference with Petroleum Administration for War.
>> Office of War Information.
> October, November, Canol Project.

November. Industrial tractors.
        Perishable tools.
        Conversion.
December. Wooden barges.
        Motor trucks.
        Los Angeles Shipbuilding and Dry Dock Corp.
        Lumber.

1944.

January. Overseas subcommittee.
        Hotel acquisitions—Navy Department.
February. Lend-lease.
        Hotel acquisitions—War Department.
March, April. Liberty ships.
March. Magnesium.
March, April. Small arms.
        Shipbuilding.
May, June, July, August. Corrigan, Osburne & Wells.
June. Paper and pulp.
August. The Breakers Hotel.
        Materials scarcity.
September, November. Surplus commodities.
September. Ark-Les Switch Corp.
September, November. Wright Aeronautical Corp.
November. Plane crash at Eglin Field, Florida.
        Automobile spare parts.
        Ammunition.
December. Maran Army Air Base.

1945.

January, March, July. Surplus property disposal.
January, February, June, July. Overseas subcommittee.
January, February, March, May, June. Manpower.
February, March. Canol Project.
March, May, July. Reconversion.
March. Great Lakes shipping.
        Food cave, Atchison, Kansas.
April, May, July. Carbon black—WPB.
April, May. Machine tools.
May, October, December. Overseas surplus property.
May. War and Navy Departments.
June, July. Curtiss-Wright Corp.
July. Aviation—transatlantic routes.
        Goodyear and Firestone strikes.
July, October, December. Transportation.

July. Army Exchange Service.
>War Shipping Administration.
>Pan American Highway.

August. Lumber.
>Airplanes in the Army Air Forces program.

September, October, November. Surplus property disposal.
September. Reorganization of Navy Yards.
>Army discharge procedure.

October. Navy discharge procedure.
>Personnel demobilization.

November. Strategic reserves.
>Navy standby plant.

1946.
>January, February. Surplus property.
>February, March, August, September, November. Foreign surplus.
>April, November. Military government in Germany.
>May. Navy supply in Hawaii.
>June, July. Erie Basin Metal Products Co.
>July, November. War profits.
>November. Housing.

1947.
>February, March. Kaiser-Hughes flying-boat contract.
>March. Inspector-General, War Department.
>June, July, August, October, November. Hughes Tool Co.
>September, December. Foreign surplus.
>September. Continental Aviation and Engineering Corp.
>October. Petroleum arrangements with Saudi Arabia.
>December. Aircraft procurement contracts.

1948.
>January. International Latex Corp.
>February. Plancor 257, Republic Steel Corp.
>February. Plancor 291, Kalunite, Inc.

BIBLIOGRAPHY

BOOKS

Bailey, Stephen K. *Congress Makes a Law*. New York: Columbia University Press, 1950.

———, and Howard D. Samuel. *Congress at Work*. New York: Henry Holt & Co., 1952.

Baldwin, Hanson W. *The Price of Power*. New York: Harper & Brothers, 1947.

Barrett, Edward L., Jr. *The Tenney Committee* (Ithaca: Cornell University Press, 1951).

Barth, Alan. *Government by Investigation*. New York: Viking Press, 1955.

Bradley, Omar N. *A Soldier's Story*. New York: Henry Holt & Co., 1951.

Brigante, John E. *The Feasibility Dispute*. Washington: Committee on Public Administration Cases. 1950.

Byrnes, James F. *Speaking Frankly*. New York: Harper & Brothers, 1947.

Carr, Robert K. *The House Committee on Un-American Activities, 1945–1950*. Ithaca: Cornell University Press, 1952.

Catton, Bruce. *The War Lords of Washington*. New York: Harcourt, Brace & Co., 1948.

Chamberlain, Lawrence H. *Loyalty and Legislative Action*. Ithaca: Cornell University Press, 1951.

Childs, Marquis W. *I Write from Washington*. New York: Harper & Brothers, 1942.

Clemens, Cyril. *The Man from Missouri*. Webster Groves: The International Mark Twain Society, 1945.

Cline, Ray S. *Washington Command Post: The Operations Division*. Office of the Chief of Military History. Washington: Government Printing Office, 1951.

Committee on Civil-Military Relations Research of the Social Science Research Council. *Civil-Military Relations: An Annotated Bibliography 1940–1952*. New York: Columbia University Press, 1954.

Connery, Robert H. *The Navy and the Industrial Mobilization in World War II*. Princeton: Princeton University Press, 1951.

Countryman, Vern. *Un-American Activities in the State of Washington*. Ithaca: Cornell University Press, 1951.

Daniels, Jonathan. *The Man of Independence*. Philadelphia: J. B. Lippincott Co., 1950.

Eaton, Richard, and La Valle Hart. *Meet Harry S Truman.* Washington: Dumbarton House, 1945.

Eisenhower, Dwight D. *Crusade in Europe.* New York: Doubleday & Co., 1948.

Fesler, James W., *et al. Industrial Mobilization for War—History of the War Production Board and Predecessor Agencies, 1940–45: Program and Administration.* Washington: Government Printing Office, 1947.

Freeman, J. Leiper. *The Political Process: Executive Bureau-Legislative Committee Relations.* New York: Doubleday & Co., 1955.

Harris, Joseph P. *The Advice and Consent of the Senate.* Berkeley: University of California Press, 1953.

Helm, William P. *Harry Truman: A Political Biography.* New York: Duell, Sloan and Pearce, 1947.

Herring, Pendleton. *The Impact of War.* New York: Farrar & Rinehart, 1941.

Howard, L. Vaughn, and Hugh A. Bone. *Current American Government: Wartime Developments.* New York: Appleton-Century Co., 1943.

Huzar, Elias. *The Purse and the Sword.* Ithaca: Cornell University Press, 1950.

Janeway, Eliot. *The Struggle for Survival.* New Haven: Yale University Press, 1951.

Koenig, Louis William. *The Presidency and the Crisis.* New York: King's Crown Press, 1944.

Leahy, William D. *I Was There.* New York: McGraw-Hill Book Co., 1950.

Lever, Harry, and Joseph Young. *Wartime Racketeers.* New York: G. P. Putnam's Sons, 1945.

Lubell, Samuel. *The Future of American Politics.* New York: Harper & Brothers, 1952.

McGeary, M. Nelson. *The Developments of Congressional Investigative Power.* New York: Columbia University Press, 1940.

McNaughton, Frank, and Walter Hehmeyer. *This Man Truman.* New York: McGraw-Hill Book Co., 1945.

Miller, John Perry. *The Pricing of Military Procurements.* New Haven: Yale University Press, 1949.

Merton, Robert K., *et al.* (eds.). *Reader in Bureaucracy.* Glencoe: The Free Press, 1952.

Millett, John D. *The Organization and Role of the Army Service Forces.* Office of the Chief of Military History. Washington: Government Printing Office, 1954.

Millis, Walter (ed.). *These Are the Generals.* New York: Alfred A. Knopf, 1943.

The Navy: A Study in Administration. Public Administration Service Publication No. 95. Reprinted from *Public Administration Review,* Autumn 1945. Chicago: Public Administration Service, 1945.

Nelson, Donald M. *Arsenal of Democracy.* New York: Harcourt, Brace & Company, 1946.

Novick, David, M. L. Anshen, and W. C. Truppner. *Wartime Production Controls.* New York: Columbia University Press, 1949.

Ogden, August Raymond. *The Dies Committee.* Washington: Catholic University Press, 1945.

Osborn, Richard C. *The Renegotiation of War Contracts.* Bulletin No. 67, Bureau of Economic and Business Research, University of Illinois. Urbana: University of Illinois, 1948.

Peltason, Jack. *The Reconversion Controversy.* Washington: Committee on Public Administration Cases, 1950.

Roosevelt, Elliott (ed.). *F.D.R.: His Personal Letters 1928–1945.* Vol. II. New York: Duell, Sloan & Pearce, 1950.

Rosenman, Samuel I. (ed.). *The Public Papers and Addresses of Franklin D. Roosevelt.* 1942 Vol., 1943 Vol., 1944–45 Vol. New York: Harper & Brothers, 1950.

Sherwood, Robert E. *Roosevelt and Hopkins.* New York: Harper & Brothers, 1948.

Smith, Louis. *American Democracy and Military Power.* Chicago: University of Chicago Press, 1951.

Somers, Herman Miles. *Presidential Agency.* Cambridge: Harvard University Press, 1950.

Stein, Harold. *Problems in Business and Industrial Mobilization: Government Organization for Economic Mobilization.* Business Information Bulletin No. 15, School of Business, University of Indiana. Bloomington: University of Indiana.

Stimson, Henry L., and McGeorge Bundy. *On Active Service in Peace and War.* New York: Harper & Brothers, 1948.

Stone, I. F. *Business As Usual: The First Year of Defense.* New York: Modern Age Books, 1941.

Taylor, Telford. *Grand Inquest.* New York: Simon & Schuster, 1955.
Toulmin, Harry Aubrey, Jr. *Diary of Democracy.* New York: Richard R. Smith, 1947.
Turner, Gordon B. (ed.). *A History of Military Affairs in Western Society since the Eighteenth Century.* New York: Harcourt, Brace & Co., 1953.
Truman, Harry S *Year of Decision.* New York: Doubleday & Co., 1955.

Wilson, H. H. *Congress: Corruption and Compromise.* New York: Rinehart & Co., 1951.
Worsley, Thomas Blanchard. *Wartime Economic Stabilization and the Efficiency of Government Procurement.* National Security Resources Board. Washington: Government Printing Office, 1949.

Young, Roland. *Congressional Politics in the Second World War.* New York: Columbia University Press, 1956.

PUBLIC DOCUMENTS

U.S. Army Service Forces. *Annual Report, Fiscal Year 1943.* Washington: Government Printing Office, 1943.
———. *Annual Report, Fiscal Year 1944.* Washington: Government Printing Office, 1944.
———. *Annual Report, Fiscal Year 1945.* Washington: Government Printing Office, 1945.
———. *Final Report.* Washington: Government Printing Office, 1946.
U.S. Bureau of the Budget. *The United States at War.* Washington: Government Printing Office, 1946.
U.S. Civilian Production Administration. *Development of the Reconversion Policies of the War Production Board,* by J. Carlyle Sitterson. Special Study No. 15. Washington: Civilian Production Administration, 1946.
———. *Dollar-A-Year and Without Compensation Personnel Policies of the War Production Board and Predecessor Agencies,* by James A. McAleer. Special Study No. 27. Washington: Civilian Production Administration, 1947.
———. *Landing Craft and the War Production Board,* by George E. Mowry. Special Study No. 11. Washington: Civilian Production Administration, 1946.
———. *Minutes of the Advisory Commission to the Council of National*

Defense, June 12, 1940 to October 22, 1941. Documentary Publication No. 1. Washington: Government Printing Office, 1946.

———. *Minutes of the Council of the Office of Production Management, December 21, 1940 to January 14, 1942.* Documentary Publication No. 2. Washington: Government Printing Office, 1946.

———. *Minutes of the Supply Priorities and Allocations Board, September 2, 1941 to January 15, 1942.* Documentary Publication No. 3. Washington: Government Printing Office, 1946.

———. *Minutes of the War Production Board, January 20, 1942 to October 9, 1945.* Documentary Publication No. 4. Washington: Government Printing Office, 1946.

U.S. Commission on Organization of the Executive Branch of the Government. *The National Security Organization.* A report to the Congress, February 1949. Washington: Government Printing Office, 1949.

———. *National Security Organization.* Appendix G. Report of the Task Force prepared for the Commission on Organization of the Executive Branch of the Government, January 1949. Washington: Government Printing Office, 1949.

U.S. Congress. *Congressional Record.* Vols. 87–91. Washington: Government Printing Office, 1941–45.

U.S. Congress, House. Committee on Military Affairs. *Interim General Report.* House Report 2272. 77th Cong., 2nd Sess. Washington: Government Printing Office, 1942.

———. *Second General Report.* House Report 1903. 78th Cong., 2nd Sess. Washington: Government Printing Office, 1944.

U.S. Congress, House. Committee on Naval Affairs. *Preliminary Report.* House Report 1634. 77th Cong., 2nd Sess. Washington: Government Printing Office, 1942.

———. *Supplemental Report.* House Report 2371. 77th Cong., 2nd Sess. Washington: Government Printing Office, 1942.

———. *Final Report.* House Report 2056. 78th Cong., 2nd Sess. Washington: Government Printing Office, 1944.

———. *Report.* House Report 2741, 79th Cong., 2nd Sess. Washington: Government Printing Office, 1947.

U.S. Congress, House. Select Committee Investigating National Defense Migration. *Third Interim Report.* House Report 1879. 77th Cong., 2nd Sess. Washington: Government Printing Office, 1942.

———. *Fifth Interim Report.* House Report 2396. 77th Cong., 2nd Sess., Washington: Government Printing Office, 1942.

———. *Sixth Interim Report.* House Report 2589. 77th Cong., 2nd Sess. Washington: Government Printing Office, 1942.

———. *Final Report.* House Report 3. 78th Cong., 1st Sess. Washington: Government Printing Office, 1943.

U.S. Congress, Senate. Special Committee Investigating the National Defense Program. *Hearings.* Parts 1–43. Washington: Government Printing Office, 1941–47. (See Appendix V for list.)

——. Reports. Senate Report 480, 77th Cong.; Senate Report 10, 78th Cong.; Senate Report 110, 79th Cong.; Senate Report 440, 80th Cong. Washington: Government Printing Office, 1941–48. (See Appendix IV for list.)

U.S. Congress, Joint Committee on Organization of Congress, Pursuant to H. Con. Res. 18, 79th Cong. *Organization of Congress Hearings.* Washington: Government Printing Office, 1945.

U.S. General Services Administration. National Archives. *Federal Records of World War II.* Vol. I, Civilian Agencies; Vol. II, Military Agencies. Washington: Government Printing Office, 1951.

——. *Records of the Special Committee of the Senate to Investigate the National Defense Program.* Preliminary Investories, No. 48. Washington: Government Printing Office, 1952.

U.S. Smaller War Plants Corporation. *Economic Concentration and World War II.* Report to the Senate Special Committee to Study the Problems of American Small Business. Senate Document 206. 79th Cong., 2nd Sess. Washington: Government Printing Office, 1946.

U.S. War Production Board. War Production in 1944. Report of the Chairman of the War Production Board, June 1945. Washington: Government Printing Office, 1945.

——. *Wartime Production Achievements and the Reconversion Outlook.* Report of the Chairman of the War Production Board, October 9, 1945. Washington: Government Printing Office, 1945.

REPORTS

Baruch, Bernard M., and John M. Hancock. *Report on War and Post-War Adjustment Policy.* Senate Document 154. 78th Cong., 2nd Sess. Washington: Government Printing Office, 1944.

Byrnes, James F. *Problems of Mobilization and Reconversion.* First Report of the Director of War Mobilization and Reconversion. Washington: Government Printing Office, 1945.

Eberstadt, Ferdinand. *Report on Unification of the War and Navy Departments.* Senate Committee on Naval Affairs print. 79th Cong., 1st Sess. Washington: Government Printing Office, 1945.

Marshall, George C. *General Marshall's Report: The Winning of the War in Europe and the Pacific.* Biennial Report of the Chief of Staff, 1943–45. New York: Simon & Schuster, 1945.

Seward, Herbert L. *Report to the Secretary of the Navy on the Tank Lighter Program of the Navy Department.* Senate Naval Affairs Committee Print. 77th Cong., 2nd Sess. Washington: Government Printing Office, 1942.

ARTICLES

"The Case Against the 77th Congress," *Fortune,* May, 1942, pp. 72 ff.

Clay, Lucius D. "Army Supply Problem," *Fortune,* February, 1943, pp. 96 ff.

"Concentration or Confusion?" *Fortune,* January, 1943, pp. 104 ff.

Dilliard, Irving. "Congressional Investigations: The Role of the Press," *The University of Chicago Law Review,* XVIII (1951), 585–90.

Finer, Herman. "Congressional Investigations: The British System," *The University of Chicago Law Review,* XVIII (1951), pp. 521–70.

Fischer, John. "The Army Takes Over," *Harper's,* May, 1945, pp. 481–91.

Fox, William T. R. "Civilians, Soldiers, and American Military Policy," *World Politics,* VII (1955), pp. 402–18.

Fulbright, J. William. "Congressional Investigations: Significance for the Legislative Process," *The University of Chicago Law Review,* XVIII (1951), pp. 440–48.

Galloway, George. "Congressional Investigation: Proposed Reforms," *The University of Chicago Law Review,* XVIII (1951), pp. 478–502.

"If This *Is* a People's War," *Fortune,* January, 1943, pp. 96 ff.

Junz, Alfred. "Congressional Investigating Committees," *Social Forces,* XXI (1954), pp. 379–410.

Marx, Fritz Morstein. "Congressional Investigations: Significance for the Administrative Process," *The University of Chicago Law Review,* XVIII (1951), pp. 503–20.

McCune, Wesley, and John R. Beal, "The Job That Made Truman President," *Harper's,* June, 1945, pp. 616–21.

McGeary, Nelson M. "Congressional Investigations During Franklin D. Roosevelt's First Term," *American Political Science Review,* XXXI (1937), pp. 680–94.

———. "Congressional Investigations: Historical Development," *The University of Chicago Law Review,* XVIII (1951), pp. 425–39.

———. "The Congressional Power of Investigation," *Nebraska Law Review,* XXVIII (1949), pp. 516–29.

Meader, George. "Congressional Investigations: Importance of the Fact-Finding Process," *The University of Chicago Law Review,* XVIII (1951), pp. 449–54.

Meader, George. "Limitations on Congressional Investigation," *Michigan Law Review,* XLVII (1949), pp. 775–86.

Neuberger, Richard L. "The Great Canol Fiasco," *The American Mercury,* April, 1948, pp. 415–21.

O'Brian, John Lord, and Fleischmann, Manly. "The War Production Board: Administrative Policies and Procedures," *George Washington Law Review,* XIII (1944), pp. 1–60.

"Report on Baruch," *Fortune,* November, 1942, pp. 98 ff.

"Retreat from the Pentagon," *Fortune,* March, 1944, pp. 133 ff.

Rogers, Lindsay. "Congressional Investigations: The Problem and Its Solution," *The University of Chicago Law Review,* XVIII, (1951), pp. 464–77

"Services of Supply," *Fortune,* September, 1942, pp. 67 ff.

Shils, Edward A. "Congressional Investigations: The Legislator and His Environment," *The University of Chicago Law Review,* XVIII (1951), pp. 571–84.

Sprout, Harold. "Trends in the Traditional Relation between Military and Civilian," *Proceedings of the American Philosophical Society,* XCII (1948), pp. 264–70.

"The State of Defense," *Fortune,* April, 1941, pp. 36 ff.

Voorhis, Jerry. "Congressional Investigations: Inner Workings," *The University of Chicago Law Review,* XVIII (1951), pp. 455–63.

White, Leonard D. "Congressional Control of the Public Service," *American Political Science Review,* XXXIX (1945), pp. 1–11.

Index